LEISUR

AA

The Lake District

AA Publishing

Authors: Mike Gerrard and
John Morrison
Original photography by Ted
Bowness
Checklists, Walks and Car Tours:
Paul Barrett
Page layout: Jo Tapper

Published by AA Publishing (a trading name of Automobile Association Developments Limited, whose registered office is Millstream, Maidenhead Road, Windsor, Berkshire, SL4 5GD. Registered Number 1878835)

First edition published 1996,
reprinted 1996, 1997, 1998.
Second edition 1999,
reprinted 2000 (twice).
Third edition 2002.

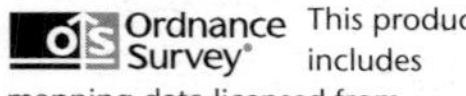

Mapping produced by the Cartographic Department of The Automobile Association. A00691.

ISBN 07495 3295 5

A CIP catalogue record for this book is available from the British Library.

Gazetteer map references are taken from the National Grid and can be used in conjunction with Ordnance Survey maps and atlases. Places featured in this guide will not necessarily be found on the maps at the back of the book.

All the walks are on rights of way, permissive paths or on routes where de facto access for walkers is accepted. On routes which are not on legal rights of way, but where access for walkers is allowed by local agreements, no implication of a right of way is intended.

The contents of this book are believed correct at the time of printing. Nevertheless, the publishers cannot accept responsibility for errors or omissions, or for changes in details given in this guide or for the consequences of any reliance on the information it provides. We have tried to ensure accuracy in this book, but things do change and we would be grateful if readers would advise us of any inaccuracies they may encounter.

Visit the AA Publishing website at www.theAA.com

Colour reproduction by L C Repro

Printed and bound by G. Canale & C. S.P.A., Torino, Italy

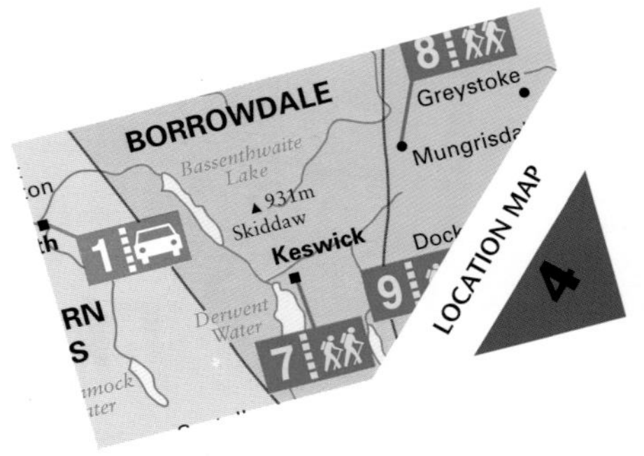

Contents

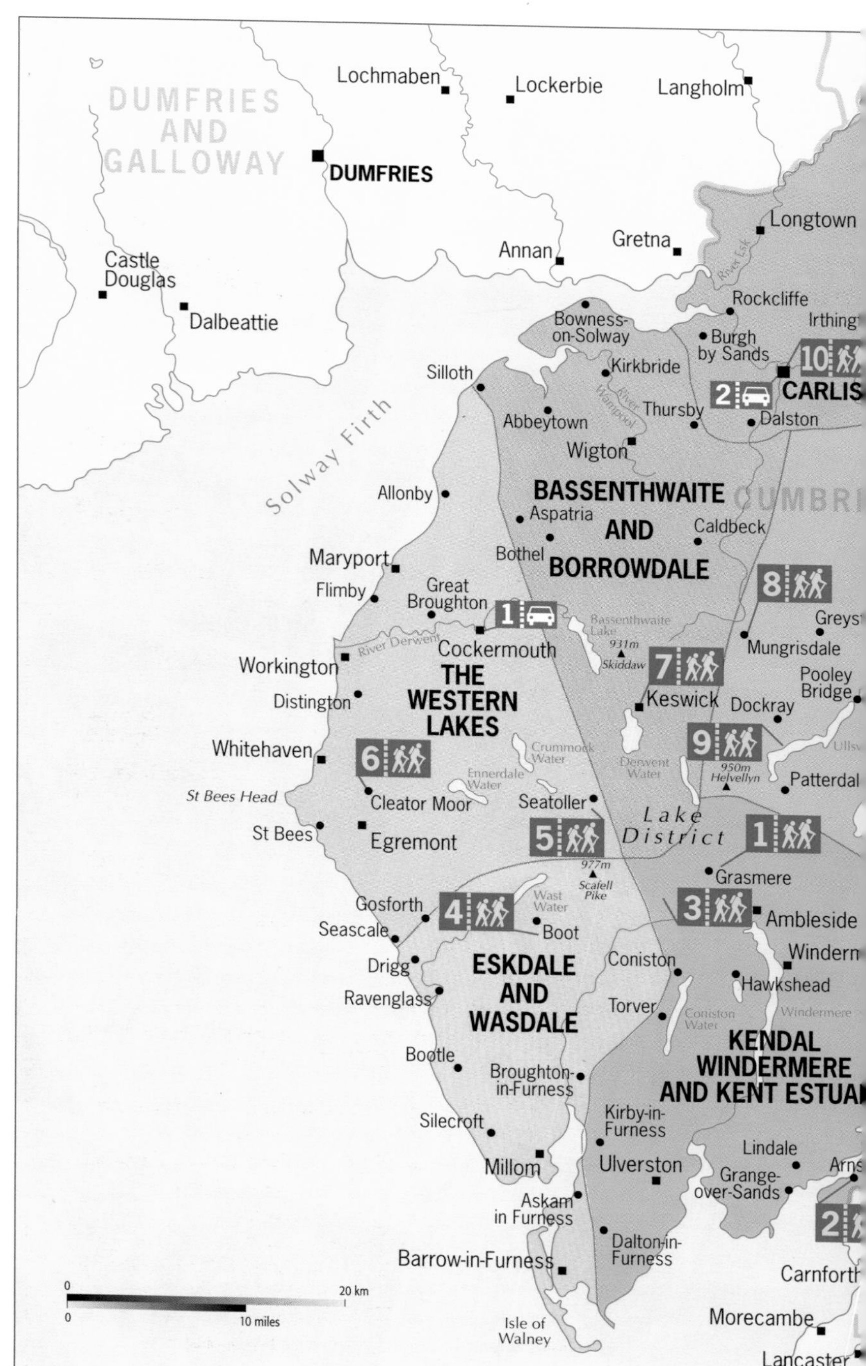

DUMFRIES AND GALLOWAY
Lochmaben
Lockerbie
Langholm
DUMFRIES
Longtown
Castle Douglas
Dalbeattie
Annan
Gretna
River Esk
Rockcliffe
Bowness-on-Solway
Burgh by Sands
Irthing
10
CARLIS
2
Silloth
Kirkbride
River Wampool
Thursby
Dalston
Abbeytown
Wigton
Solway Firth
Allonby
BASSENTHWAITE AND BORROWDALE
CUMBRI
Aspatria
Caldbeck
Bothel
Maryport
Flimby
Great Broughton
1
8
Greys
Bassenthwaite Lake
931m
Skiddaw
Mungrisdale
River Derwent
Cockermouth
Workington
THE WESTERN LAKES
7
Keswick
Pooley Bridge
Distington
Dockray
Whitehaven
6
Crummock Water
Derwent Water
9
950m
Helvellyn
Ennerdale Water
Patterdal
St Bees Head
Cleator Moor
Seatoller
St Bees
Egremont
5
Lake District
1
977m
Scafell Pike
Grasmere
Gosforth
4
Wast Water
3
Ambleside
Seascale
Boot
Drigg
ESKDALE AND WASDALE
Coniston
Winderm
Hawkshead
Ravenglass
Torver
Coniston Water
Windermere
KENDAL WINDERMERE AND KENT ESTUA
Bootle
Broughton-in-Furness
Silecroft
Kirby-in-Furness
Lindale
Millom
Ulverston
Grange-over-Sands
Arns
Askam in Furness
2
Dalton-in-Furness
Barrow-in-Furness
Carnforth
0
20 km
0
10 miles
Isle of Walney
Morecambe
Lancaster

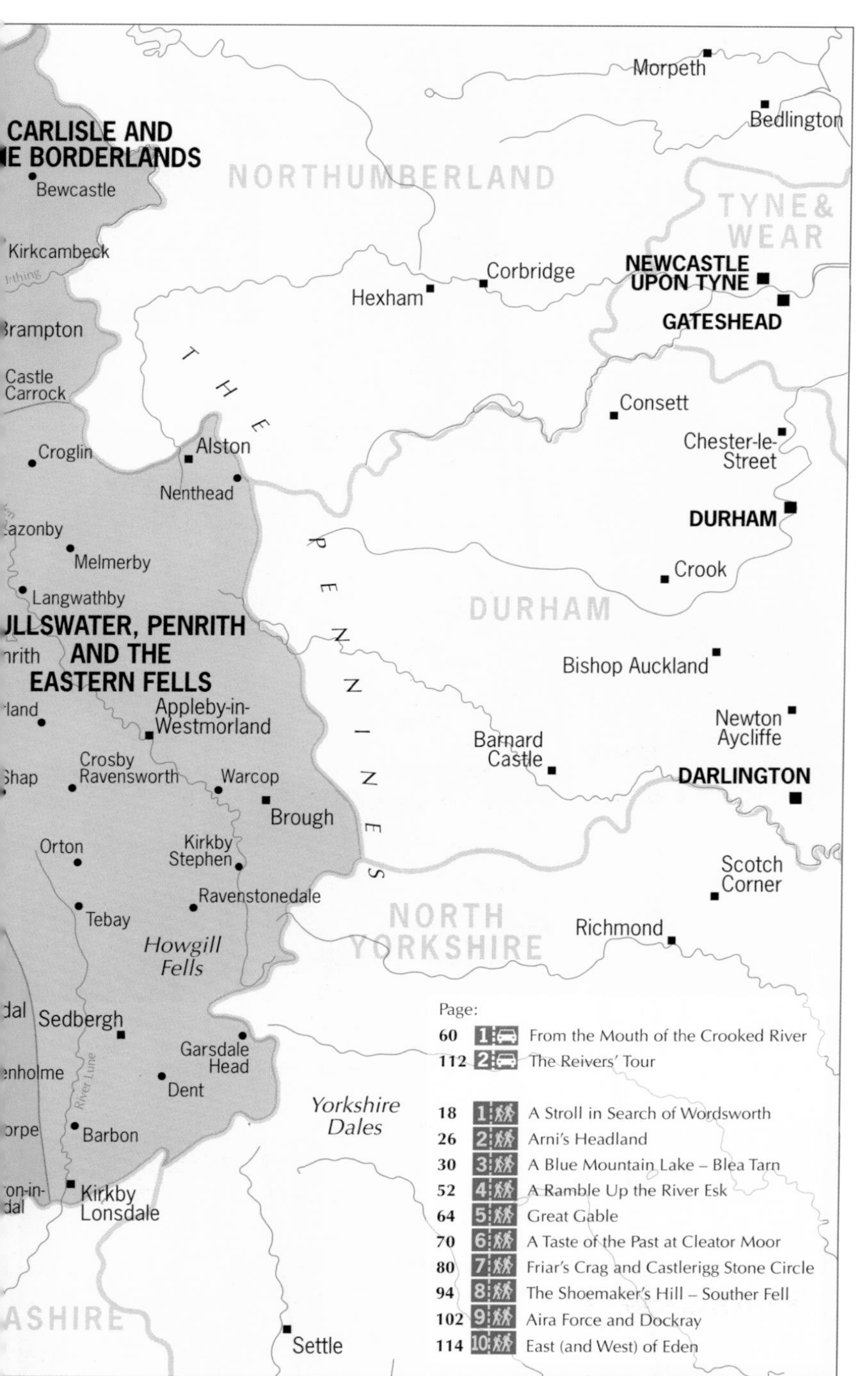

Page:

60	1	From the Mouth of the Crooked River
112	2	The Reivers' Tour
18	1	A Stroll in Search of Wordsworth
26	2	Arni's Headland
30	3	A Blue Mountain Lake – Blea Tarn
52	4	A Ramble Up the River Esk
64	5	Great Gable
70	6	A Taste of the Past at Cleator Moor
80	7	Friar's Crag and Castlerigg Stone Circle
94	8	The Shoemaker's Hill – Souther Fell
102	9	Aira Force and Dockray
114	10	East (and West) of Eden

Introducing the Lake District

The Lake District is Britain's premier scenic area. The lakes, fells and mountains were shaped by melting and bursting rocks in the unimaginable heat of millions of years ago, slaked by the sea, smothered in dust-storms and sculpted by deluge and glacier.

There are three scenic types: in the south the softer tree-clad landscape of the Silurian slates; in the north the angular landscape formed from the shales of the ancient sedimentary Skiddaw slates; in the centre, the craggy heights of the Borrowdale volcanic series. The enclosure of the open fells with dry-stone walls, creating a pattern of fields, took place during 1750–1850.

No rural area is richer in literary associations – Wordsworth; Coleridge; Ruskin; Beatrix Potter; Arthur Ransome and Melvyn Bragg have all made their home here and many more visited.

Today the Lakes are sure to refresh mind and body of all who come.

HUNTING
Left, this is John Peel country, so listen out for the deep baying of hounds a-hunting among the fells

GRASMERE GINGERBREAD
Above, the delectable, fragrant Grasmere Gingerbread has been made to Sarah Nelson's secret recipe for years

WORDSWORTH
William Wordsworth's awe and admiration of his native landscape, expressed in verse, did much to attract early tourists to the region in the 19th century when the popularity of the Lake District grew rapidly

THE RAVENGLASS AND ESKDALE RAILWAY
Let the little train take the strain and enjoy the narrow-gauge fun of the Ravenglass and Eskdale Railway, above

CUMBERLAND WRESTLING
No, it's not a Superman look-alike contest, but a bout of the traditional, highly skilled Cumberland Wrestling, left

MINING
Not just a pretty place, Cumbria has a tradition of mining and industry, right

RUSKIN AND BRANTWOOD
The important critic and social commentator John Ruskin purchased Brantwood in 1871, and today it contains a fascinating collection relating to his life and work

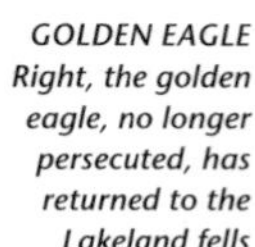

GOLDEN EAGLE
Right, the golden eagle, no longer persecuted, has returned to the Lakeland fells

LAKELAND FLORA
Above, Cumbria embraces a rich variety of vegetation in a landscape that ranges from sandy seashore to rocky mountainside

TEN VILLAGE NAMES TO PONDER

Blindcrake
Boot
Catlowdy
Carkettle
Hoff
Holebigerrah
Horace
Knock
Unthank
Whelpo

THE ESSENTIAL LAKE DISTRICT

If you have little time and you want to sample the essence of the Lake District:

Visit Dove Cottage (but not in high season), Wordsworth's home in Grasmere... **Gaze** across Tarn Hows towards the beautiful backdrop of rolling hills and the Langdale Pikes... **Steam along** the scenic Haverthwaite–Lakeside Railway followed by a leisurely cruise on Windermere... **Negotiate** the twists and turns (and the 1-in-3/33% gradient) of the spectacular Hardknott Pass... **Walk** round Buttermere and enjoy stunning views in all directions, then continue to the impressive waterfall of Scale Force... **Discover** The Sheep and Wool Centre at Cockermouth, then go on to mingle with the mountain climbers and country walkers in the town.

A LEISURELY WAY TO TRAVEL
Sailing on the larger lakes is a popular pastime, and can be practised in style on one of the leisurely old steamers, above

WALKING
Visitors come to the Lake District for the magnificent hilltop views, left, so park the car and explore on foot

CYCLING
Cycling in these hills, on designated tracks, is a challenge for all the family, right

A Weekend in the Lakes: Day One

For many people a weekend break or a long weekend is a popular way of spending their leisure time.
These four pages offer a loosely planned itinerary designed to ensure that you make the most of your time, what ever the weather, and see and enjoy the very best the area has to offer. Places with gazetteer entries are in **bold.**

Friday Night

Stay in or near **Windermere** – at Gilpin Lodge Country House Hotel if you can afford it! This delightful hotel, set in 20 acres of gardens and woodland, has country-style bedrooms with some beautiful four-poster and brass beds.

Saturday Morning

Cross Windermere using the ferry service from **Bowness**, then follow the B5285 to visit Beatrix Potter's House, Hill Top, at **Near Sawrey**. Several of her 'little books' were written in this small 17th-century house.

Continue north on the B5285 to **Ambleside**, one of the major centres of the Lakes and an excellent place to shop for souvenirs.

If you are in Ambleside on the first Saturday in July, don't miss the rushbearing ceremony when children carry rushes around the town.

Revisit a world of childhood at Near Sawrey, above

Left, hear the water thunder at Stock Ghyll, Ambleside

Above, visit Wordsworth's beautiful garden at Rydal Mount

Right, take in charming Grasmere, and watch the delightful daffodils dance in season, below

Saturday Lunch

A good place for lunch is the Drunken Duck at Barngates, which is signposted off the B5286 Hawkshead–Ambleside road. It offers a relaxed atmosphere and good food.

Saturday Afternoon

Drive north on the A591 for Grasmere and Keswick. Visit **Rydal Mount**, where William Wordsworth lived from 1813 until his death in 1850. The house, which contains family portraits and many of the poet's personal possessions, is situated in beautiful gardens overlooking Rydal Water.

Continue on the A591 to **Grasmere.** Explore the village, which has a National Park Information Centre, and then make your way to Dove Cottage and the adjacent barn – now the Wordsworth Museum.

Saturday Night

There is plenty of accommodation in Grasmere to suit all pockets, but for something really special stay at Michael's Nook Country House set on the hills above Grasmere. This outstanding hotel is furnished with fine antiques and serves impressive gourmet meals.

A Weekend in the Lakes: Day Two

Our second and final day in the Lakes offers an excellent walk in the morning and a drive that visits a waterfall, the area's second largest lake and its highest pass. If the start of the day is wet then the morning could be spent in Keswick.

unday Morning

If it is wet then drive straight to Keswick.

If the weather is fine then it is time to discover the delights of the Lake District on foot. Our Walk on page 18 (2–3 hours, 3½ miles/5.6km) starts at Dove Cottage and leads to **Rydal Mount** before returning along the shore of Rydal Water.

On completing the walk, drive on the A591 to Keswick, passing the waters of Thirlmere on your left and the heights of Helvellyn on your right.

unday Lunch

Keswick is the heart of the northern Lake District. A happy (wet) morning could be spent browsing round the tempting shops. Visit the Pencil Museum (more interesting than you might expect), the Cars of the Stars Motor Museum, or discover the unexpected treasures of Keswick Museum.

When it is time for lunch look out for The Packhorse Inn in the town centre, an attractive and comfortable pub which welcomes children.

Go souvenir-hunting in Keswick, above

Dove Cottage, left, is the start point for our Walk

Enjoy the vintage machinery of the Pencil Museum, below

Search out wild daffodils by Ullswater's shore, right

Look up Townend house at Troutbeck, below

Sunday Afternoon

After lunch leave Keswick on the A66 travelling east. Turn right on to the A5091 heading down towards Aira Force (National Trust), a series of splendid waterfalls in a spectacular gorge, with an arboretum, a café and a landscaped Victorian park. Leave the car park and travel south on the A592 along the western shore of **Ullswater** (the second largest lake in the Lake District), passing through the popular tourist villages of Glenridding and Patterdale.

Continue on the A592 to travel the spectacular **Kirkstone Pass** (the highest road pass in the Lake District) to return to Windermere.

Just before reaching Windermere detour through the village of **Troutbeck** and visit Townend, a 17th-century wealthy yeoman farmer's house.

Take in the delights of busy lake Windermere, right

Kendal, Windermere and the Kent Estuary

For many visitors a trip to 'the Lakes' means joining the bustling crowds in Kendal, Bowness or Windermere. While these towns offer plenty to see and do, they are tourist 'honeypots' and can become overcrowded in the high season. Conversely, there are fascinating towns and villages in south Lakeland, some looking out over Morecambe Bay, that are too often overlooked by visitors. The landscape itself, generally greener and more intimate in character than the higher Lakeland hills, offers delightful walking country in which you can find the 'quiet recreation' enshrined in the philosophy of the National Park.

AMBLESIDE MUSEUM

Founded as a library in 1909 by the Armitt sisters, this is now a fine small museum illustrating the life and work of writers and artists such as John Ruskin, Beatrix Potter and the Collingwoods. The collection includes most of Beatrix Potter's scientific illustrations as well as pictures by noted artists such as William Green and J B Pyne.

AMBLESIDE Map ref NY3704

Lying at the northern tip of lake Windermere, Ambleside is a convenient base for touring the central Lakes, with Grasmere and the Langdale valleys just a short drive away. The town has adopted this role with gusto; it seems that every other shop sells walking boots, outdoor clothing and Kendal Mint Cake.

The town began to prosper during Queen Victoria's reign, with the growth of tourism. Many centuries earlier the Romans saw the strategic potential of this site, and built a fort they called *Galava* close to where the rivers Brathay and Rothay combine and flow into Windermere.

Ambleside won its market charter in 1650, and a few buildings – including a watermill – survive from this time. However, the best-known building in Ambleside is also the smallest: the delightful Bridge House, built on a little bridge that spans the beck of Stock Ghyll. It must be one of the most photographed buildings in the Lake District. Thought to have been built by the owners of Ambleside Hall, perhaps as a folly or apple store, Bridge House now serves as a diminutive National Trust information centre.

William Wordsworth was familiar with Ambleside as a market town. For a few years, while he held the post of Distributor of Stamps for Westmorland, he had an office here. A mural in the parish church depicts the rushbearing ceremony, which is still celebrated on the first Saturday in July. The origins of this event lie in medieval times, when people used rushes as floor coverings in their dwellings and put fresh new rushes down each year.

It is just a short walk from the centre of Ambleside to the lake at Waterhead. Like a Bowness Bay in miniature, with a short stretch of beach, dinghies for hire and ever-hungry ducks, Waterhead is a favourite spot at holiday times. The steamers *Swan, Tern* and *Teal* call in at Waterhead on their round-the-lake cruises.

A walk in the opposite direction, following Stock Ghyll through woodland, will bring you to Stock Ghyll Force, an entrancing waterfall. 'Force' is a corruption of 'foss', the old Norse word for waterfall.

TRADITIONAL SPORTS

Traditional Lakeland sports are held at Ambleside on the Thursday before the first Monday in August. Events include fell racing, hound trails and Cumberland and Westmorland wrestling.

The diminutive Bridge House is a favourite Lakeland landmark

The square tower of Cartmel's priory church is unusually set on the diagonal

DARING EXPLOITS
The collection at Holker Hall Lakeland Motor Museum incorporates an exhibition featuring the record-breaking exploits of the remarkable Campbells, Sir Malcolm (1885–1948) and his son Donald (1921–67), whose adventures on land and water thrilled the world. There are full-size replicas of their futuristic cars and boats, and a video shows the moment on Coniston Water when *Bluebird* flipped into the air and broke up when Donald Campbell was attempting to raise the water speed record beyond 300mph (480kph).

CARTMEL Map ref SD3878

First-time visitors will wonder why a village as small as Cartmel should be blessed with such a large and magnificent church. In the 12th century when Cartmel (along with Carlisle and Lanercost) was chosen as the site for an Augustinian priory, the original endowment stipulated that local people should always have the right to worship in the priory church. When the monastery itself was disbanded by the Dissolution in 1536–7 the priory church was saved.

Much of the stone from the priory was re-used to build what is now the village of Cartmel, and the only other tangible relic of monastic times is the gatehouse (in the care of the National Trust, now a heritage centre) that forms one side of the little market square. The stepped market cross stands near by, but the markets themselves are long gone. The Cartmel of today is a pretty little village, worth exploring in its own right as well as for its gem of a church.

To the south of the village is Holker Hall, the home of the Cavendish family; allow plenty of time for your visit because there is a lot to see. The Hall itself retains the atmosphere of a family home, not least because you are free to explore the rooms unhindered by ropes and barriers. The 25 acres of formal gardens and woodland are justifiably famous.

Extensive outbuildings now house the Lakeland Motor Museum, where devotees of the internal combustion engine will find a fascinating collection of historic cars and other vehicles, from the early days of motoring to the present.

CONISTON Map ref SD3097

Overlooked by the bulk of the Old Man of Coniston, 2,627 feet (801m), and near the northern tip of Coniston Water, the village enjoys a superb setting. A little off the beaten track, Coniston caters best for those who want to explore the magnificent range of peaks that rise up behind the little grey town.

It was these mountains, and the mineral wealth they yielded, which created the village of Coniston. While copper had been mined in this area since Roman times the industry grew most rapidly during the 18th and 19th centuries and the village expanded accordingly. The story of copper mining, slate quarrying and farming, as well as of celebrities such as John Ruskin, Arthur Ransome and Donald Campbell, are told in the Ruskin Museum. Situated in the village since 1901, it has been splendidly revitalised.

A short stroll from the centre of Coniston brings you to the shore of the lake where a public slipway allows the launching of boats (no powered craft, please); sailing dinghies and windsurfers can be hired by the hour.

Few houses can enjoy a more beautiful setting than Brantwood, on the eastern shore of the lake. From 1872 to 1900 this was the home of John Ruskin, artist, poet and social reformer, who became the most influential and controversial art critic of his time. Brantwood is filled with Ruskin's drawings, watercolours and other items recalling a man whose ideas influenced such intellectual giants as Mahatma Gandhi and Leo Tolstoy. He is buried in Coniston churchyard.

Tarn Hows, one of the most-visited beauty spots in the Lakes is a short drive from Coniston off the B5285 Hawkshead road. Just yards from the National Trust car park, you can gaze across the tarn, studded with islands, surrounded by conifer woodland and given the most beautiful backdrop of rolling hills. This spectacular view has graced thousands of biscuit-tin lids and calendars.

STEAM YACHT *GONDOLA*

Coniston's big success story in recent years has been the rebirth of the steam yacht *Gondola*. Originally launched in 1859, to convey tourists in some luxury she remained in service for 80 years before falling into dereliction. Her boiler was sold to a sawmill; her hull was converted into a houseboat; the winter storms of 1963 washed her ashore. In 1977 the National Trust undertook the task of rebuilding *Gondola* at the Vickers shipyard in Barrow. The interior was restored to its original upholstered splendour. Since 1980 visitors to Coniston Water have once again been able to enjoy Victorian elegance while cruising the lake. *Gondola* visits Park-a-Moor, towards the southern end of the lake, and makes a stop at Brantwood, before returning to Coniston; the delightful round trip takes about an hour.

The graceful steam yacht* Gondola *plies a summertime route on Coniston Water

Crossing the treacherous expanse of Morecambe Sands is a serious business

TREACHEROUS SANDS

Until the middle of the 19th century travellers used the route across the sands of Morecambe Bay to Grange, hence the town's Sunday-best name of Grange-over-Sands. The Romans certainly crossed the bay, as did the monks of Furness Abbey when they visited their Lancashire granges. Stagecoaches came this way, knocking hours off the overland route around the Kent estuary. The route avoiding the treacherous quicksand was notoriously difficult to find and in the 16th century the Duchy of Lancaster appointed an official guide to escort travellers safely across the shifting sands of Morecambe Bay.

GRANGE-OVER-SANDS Map ref SD4077

Looking out over Morecambe Bay is the little resort of Grange-over-Sands. With its ornamental gardens, mile-long (1.6km) promenade and relaxed ambience, the town harks back to the reign of Queen Victoria, when visitors looked for quieter pursuits than they do today. The building of the scenic Furness railway line, in 1857, brought visitors in great numbers from the industrial towns of Lancashire to south Lakeland.

Grange grew from a small village into a popular resort, as it catered for the influx of visitors. Had the town been blessed with a better beach it might even have grown to rival Morecambe, its brasher, noisier cousin just across the bay.

Thanks to the Gulf Stream, Grange enjoys a congenially mild climate, a factor which helps to explain why so many people find the town a pleasant place in which to spend their retirement years. Springtime is reckoned to be warmer in Grange than anywhere else in the north. 'Green fingered' gardeners are encouraged by the climate, and plants grow here that would be unlikely to survive elsewhere on the west coast.

GRASMERE Map ref NY3307

The village of Grasmere is central, geographically and historically, to the Lake District. Set in a valley surrounded by hills, and a short stroll from Grasmere lake, the village is a gem.

Literary pilgrims have flocked to Grasmere since the days when William Wordsworth's 'plain living and high thinking' produced some of the finest romantic poetry. It was during a walking tour of the Lake District, with his lifelong friend Samuel Taylor Coleridge, that Wordsworth first spied the little house that would become his home for eight of his most productive years (see Walk on page 18).

Despite its size, the house came to be filled with the artistic luminaries of the day, and it was here, between 1799 and 1808, that he composed some of his best-known poems. Previously an inn (the Dove and Olive Branch), Wordsworth knew the house as Town End. It was years later, after the poet's death, that it was christened Dove Cottage. The house is open to the public, and an adjacent barn has been converted into the Wordsworth Museum.

By the time Wordsworth's wife, Mary, was expecting their fourth child, Dove Cottage was becoming too small. The family moved first to Allan Bank and the Rectory (both in Grasmere, and both now private homes), before making one last move to Rydal Mount.

GRASMERE SPORTS

The famous Grasmere Sports (the first recorded meeting was in 1852), now held on the third Sunday after the first Monday in August, have become the Lake District's most celebrated event. One of the most popular sports for spectators is fell racing which involves competitors tackling an arduous route to the top of the nearest fell followed by a wild dash back down to the arena. Other events include hound trailing and Cumberland and Westmorland wrestling.

Silver Howe is reflected in the tranquil waters of Grasmere

A Stroll in Search of Wordsworth

An easy walk which explores the countryside that was an inspiration to one of the most celebrated romantic poets in the English language, William Wordsworth. The greater portion of his life was spent here, so soak up the atmosphere on a relaxed stroll in the Grasmere area from Dove Cottage to Rydal Mount.

Time: 2–3 hours. Distance: 3½ miles (5.6km).
Location: Grasmere, 3½ miles (5.6km) northwest of Ambleside off the A591.
Start: Dove Cottage on the edge of Grasmere, beside the A591. Park at one of several car parks in Grasmere. (OS grid ref: NY342070.)
OS Map: Outdoor Leisure 7 (English Lakes – South Eastern area) 1:25,000.
See Key to Walks on page 121.

ROUTE DIRECTIONS

Facing **Dove Cottage**, turn right and take the road leading uphill. The road levels and, just after a small pond on the left, curves right by Howe Top Farm. Bear left here following the smaller road uphill. Keep to this path, known as the 'Coffin Route', disregarding the waymarked path leading to Alcock Tarn. The road levels and passes a large garden behind a stone wall on the left. Soon Rydal Water comes into view to the right in the valley below. Ignore a path which forks downhill to the right, and keep ahead on the main track. At a right-hand bend ignore the path on the left going uphill and keep to the level main path. Shortly the path comes to a gate just past a cottage on the left.

Go through into woods and proceed eastwards. Eventually leave the woods behind to emerge out into open countryside. After about half an hour's walking the path descends, passing behind Rydal Mount on the right. Beyond a gate, turn right downhill on to a road, passing the entrance to **Rydal Mount** and continue past Rydal Hall on the left. In a few yards go through an iron gate on your right to visit **Rydal church** and Dora's Field. Walk from the church to the main road, turn right and continue on the pavement for 100 yards (91m) to a waymarked footpath on the left. Follow this, cross a footbridge, then at a fork of paths bear right and pass through grassland, above the river.

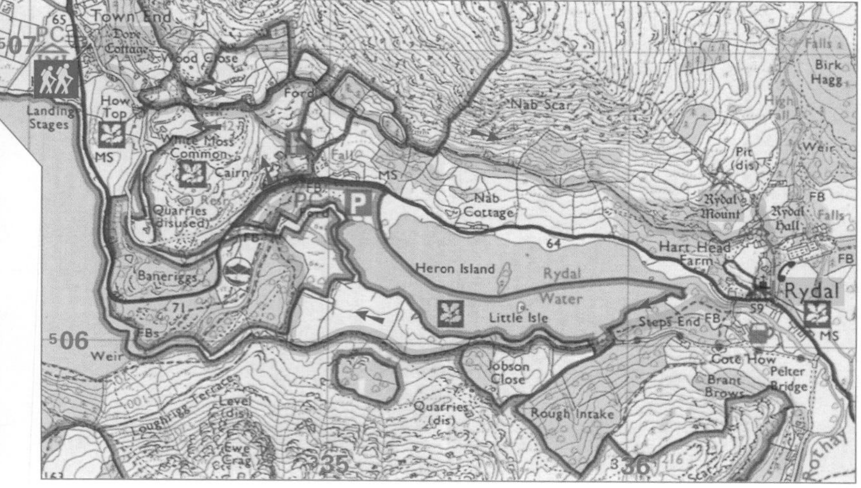

Almost hidden amid the trees and reeds, a venerable boat-house watches over Rydal Water

From here the route is easy to trace, the path enters woodland, then comes into the open beyond a gate. Continue on the lakeside path eventually following it left away from the lake, and uphill beside a wall. Pass a ruined barn and reach a narrow gate in the wall on the right between slate gateposts. On your left Ewe Crag looms high above.

Go through the gate into woodland. Follow the main path downhill, which soon bears left and levels, before continuing to a wooden bridge (ignore smaller paths branching off). Cross the bridge over the River Rothay and take the path ahead, which then bears to the right. Continue until, just before a ford and bridge, a path branches to the left. Follow this left-hand path over a footbridge and pass National Trust toilets on the left to arrive at the A591 opposite a post box.

Cross the road and take the waymarked path on the right of the post box. Enter woodland with a stream on the left and a waterfall. Where the path branches by the waterfall take the right-hand path leading uphill and shortly go through the gate ahead (with another gate on the right). Climb the narrow stony track until it joins the outward route just below a stone cottage. Turn left and follow the route back to Dove Cottage and the Wordsworth Museum and the start of the walk.

POINTS OF INTEREST

Dove Cottage and the Wordsworth Museum

Wordsworth called Grasmere 'the loveliest spot that man hath ever found'. He lived here with his family from 1799 to 1808, and during that time wrote much of his best-known poetry. The house is kept in its original condition and the museum displays various manuscripts, paintings and other items associated with the poet.

Rydal Mount

Enjoying a splendid elevated position overlooking Windermere and Rydal Water, this house was the family home of William Wordsworth from 1813 until his death in 1850. It contains an important group of family portraits, furniture, some of the poet's personal possessions and some first editions of his work.

Rydal church and Dora's Field

The Church of St Mary is where William Wordsworth and his family worshipped and the poet's pew is in front of the pulpit.
Near by is the famous Dora's Field (owned by the National Trust), a small piece of enclosed fell which Wordsworth bought and later dedicated to his daughter. He planted it with daffodils in her memory.

RECREATION IN THE FOREST
Grizedale Forest Visitor Centre illustrates the story of the forest from wild woodland to its present role as an area managed for timber, wildlife and recreation. There are waymarked walks ranging from the 1-mile (1.6-km) Ridding Wood Trail to the 9-mile (14.4-km) Silurian Way, with routes for cyclists, observation hides (the forest is home to red and roe deer) and many picnic sites.

GRIZEDALE FOREST Map ref SD3394

Controversy has long surrounded the loss of broad-leaved woodland in the Lake District and the creation of new conifer plantations. Conservationists complained that the uncompromising geometry of these new plantations looked out of place in the Lakeland landscape. William Wordsworth's was one of the voices raised about the too frequent planting of larch trees.

There was a feeling, too, that the serried ranks of pine and larch supported little wildlife, and offered too few rights of way for walkers. The Forestry Commission gradually addressed these problems, and the Grizedale estate, situated between the lakes of Coniston Water and Windermere, became the first of their forests to actively encourage a variety of recreational activities. During the 1960s the forest was opened up to the public, and a visitor centre was built; Grizedale is now the largest forest in the Lake District.

The Grizedale Forest of today combines two roles: woodland recreation and the commercial production of timber. Your first stop should be the visitor centre and the adjacent gallery, where you will learn about the forest, its calendar of events and the many recreational activities it supports. A guide to the forest details the many waymarked trails suitable for walkers and cyclists of all abilities.

An imaginative initiative brought art into the forest. Sculptors were regularly sponsored to create artworks in woodland settings; there are now more than 80 sculptures, nestling among the trees or standing alone on grassy hilltops, to amaze and amuse. There is a children's play area, mountain bike hire and a café.

Visitors will find there's nothing timid about these delightful residents of Grizedale Forest

Approaching Newby Halt on the Lakeside and Haverthwaite Railway

HAVERTHWAITE Map ref SD3483

Haverthwaite, beyond the southern tip of Windermere, is the southern terminus of the Lakeside and Haverthwaite Railway. Originally a branch of the Furness Railway, the line used to carry goods and passengers from Ulverston to connect with the Windermere steamers at Lakeside; this was one of the first attempts to encourage mass tourism in the Lake District. Four passenger steamers began service in 1850; trains began running 20 years later. Passenger numbers peaked before World War I, and the story, subsequently, was one of decline, curtailed services and finally, in 1967, closure.

A group of rail enthusiasts fought to buy the branch line and re-open it as a recreational line, using steam-hauled trains. Despite many setbacks they succeeded in taking over the 3½-mile (5.6km) stretch of line between Haverthwaite and Lakeside. The proud re-opening came in 1973; since then a full service has been maintained. As in the railway's heyday, the scenic journey can be combined with a leisurely cruise on Windermere.

Newby Bridge marks the southern limit of the lake, where it drains into the River Leven. The hotel, by the bridge, with tables overlooking the river is an ideal spot to while away an idle hour feeding the ducks. Two miles (3.2km) from Newby Bridge is Stott Park Bobbin Mill. The building, dating from 1835, is an evocative reminder of a local industry producing bobbins for the clattering textile mills of Lancashire. The raw material was timber from coppiced woodland; trees were cut back every 20 years to ensure vigorous new growth of side-shoots which could be 'turned' on hand-operated lathes.

FELL FOOT PARK

Fell Foot Park (National Trust) offers one of the few sites on Windermere's eastern shore where there is public access to the water. This 18-acre family playground offers safe bathing, boats for hire and space to spread a picnic blanket. A ferry operates between Fell Foot Park and Lakeside, where you will find the terminus of the restored railway and steamer berth as well as the Aquarium of the Lakes. The aquarium has imaginative naturalistic displays of water and bird life in rivers, lakes and nearby Morecambe Bay.

Hawkshead's finest corners are happily beyond the reach of traffic

A VISION OF THE FUTURE
William Wordsworth's love of the Lakeland landscape had more than literary repercussions. He combined his passion for the fells and lakes with an understanding of their vulnerability to damage by transport, industry and the tourists, who were just beginning to discover the awe-inspiring scenery. In *A Guide through the District of the Lakes*, he even anticipated the creation of the National Parks. He wrote of 'Persons of pure taste throughout the whole island, who, by their visits (often repeated) to the Lakes in the North of England, testify that they deem the district a sort of national property, in which every man has a right and interest who has an eye to perceive and a heart to enjoy'.

HAWKSHEAD Map ref SD3598
Achingly picturesque, Hawkshead has suffered in recent years from the influx of visitors. Though a large car park now ensures the narrow streets comprise a car-free zone, this is no place to be on a busy Bank Holiday. The village has, however, retained much of the charm that first endeared it to the young William Wordsworth, when, between 1779 and 1787, he was a pupil at the little Grammar School and lodged at the house of Ann Tyson. Years later he recalled the 'home amusements by the warm peat fire'.

It was during his schooldays that Wordsworth developed the passion for the Lakeland hills that was to fuel so much of his poetry. Ann Tyson's cottage still stands, as does the school (here you can see the desk on which the schoolboy carved his name).

Hawkshead is an intriguing maze of tiny thoroughfares, alleyways and courtyards. The white-washed houses – many 17th century – never suffered at the hands of any unimaginative town planner, and exhibit an architectural anarchy that merely adds to the charm of the village. The 15th-century parish church boasts wall frescoes, but its main charm is its position on a knoll overlooking the village.

A more recent attraction is the National Trust's Beatrix Potter Gallery, in the middle of the village, where you will find displays of her original drawings, and information about her life as author, artist, farmer and pioneer of the conservation movement.

Hawkshead was once an important market town serving a wide area, much of it owned by the monks of Furness Abbey. Only one building now remains from monastic times: the sturdy little courthouse, just north of the village.

KENDAL Map ref SD5192

For motorists coming from the M6, the first sight of Kendal, in the valley below, means that the Lakes are 'only just round the corner'. Though some motorists take the bypass without a second thought, impatient to reach Bowness or Windermere, others prefer to see what Kendal has to offer. The one-way traffic system can be frustrating; a missed turning may require a circuit of the town centre before you can find it again. It's better to explore on foot, and investigate Kendal's numerous 'yards' or alleyways.

Most people, if asked what Kendal is famous for, would offer 'K' Shoes and Kendal Mint Cake (a hard, mint-flavoured sugar slab much loved by the climbing fraternity), but it was the woollen industry that brought prosperity to this little town astride the River Kent. Indeed, the town's motto is 'Wool is my Bread'. From medieval times, when Flemish weavers settled in the town, there has been a worldwide trade in wool from the flocks of sturdy Herdwick sheep that still roam the Lakeland fells. In *Henry IV Part 1*, Shakespeare mentions archers wearing cloth of Kendal Green.

Catherine Parr, sixth wife of King Henry VIII, was born in Kendal Castle, which enjoys a splendid view over the town. The view still repays the climb, though the castle itself is in ruins.

ROBERT PHILIPSON

A sword in Kendal parish church is thought to have belonged to Robert Philipson, a Cavalier during the Civil War. While he was away, fighting in Carlisle, Roundheads laid siege to his Belle Isle house on Windermere. He sought revenge by attacking Kendal parish church when he thought the Parliamentarians were at prayer. He and his horsemen rode right into the church, brandishing their weapons. The church was empty, however, except for one unfortunate, and innocent, man who Philipson ran through with his sword.

Kendal's flower-decked Abbot Hall park offers more gentle walking terrain

A sculpture by the great 20th-century artist Barbara Hepworth stands outside the Museum of Lakeland Life

THE QUAKER TAPESTRY
In the Friend's Meeting House 77 beautifully embroidered panels, the work of 4,000 men, women and children from 15 countries, illustrate the remarkable social history of the Quaker Movement.

KENDAL'S YARDS
Kendal's alleyways, known locally as 'yards', are an integral part of the 'Auld Grey Town' and a potent reminder of when people lived with the constant threat of cross-border raids by Scottish reivers. In times of danger the townspeople of Kendal used the yards to keep their families and livestock safe. The entrances to the yards could be secured against attack.

Near the parish church (one of the largest and most imposing in the country) is Abbot Hall. This elegant Georgian house is now an equally elegant art gallery, showing works by the many artists – including Ruskin and Constable – who were inspired by the Lakeland landscape. The Museum of Lakeland Life and Industry, also at Abbot Hall, brings the recent centuries to life, with reconstructed shops, room settings and a farming display. The study of Arthur Ransome, author of *Swallows and Amazons* and many other children's books, has been painstakingly recreated.

At the opposite end of town, close to the railway station, is the Kendal Museum, with its fascinating collection of archaeolgy, geology and natural and social history, based on the collection of 'curiosities' first exhibited by William Todhunter in 1796. He charged a fee of 'one shilling per person; children and servants 6d each'. There are displays of wildlife, both local and global (though the case crammed full of iridescent humming birds does seem gross by today's standards).

One of Kendal's best-known sons was Alfred Wainwright (1907–1991), whose seven immaculately handwritten guides to the Lakeland hills became classics in his own lifetime. You can see Wainwright's little office in Kendal Museum; this is no leap of the imagination, as Wainwright held the post of honorary curator for many years. A hand-drawn map reveals that his interests were already in place at the tender age of ten. However, it wasn't until he was 45 that he began the mammoth task of writing his Pictorial Guides, which will be indispensable reading for many years to come. Other books about his beloved North Country followed, until his death in 1991.

KENTMERE Map ref NX4603

The valley of Kentmere begins at Staveley, just off the A591 between Kendal and Windermere. From Staveley the road meanders prettily along the valley bottom, northwards, never too far from the infant River Kent (which later splits the town of Kendal in two) before coming to a halt at the little village of Kentmere. The village church, St Cuthbert's, has 16th-century roof beams and a bronze memorial to Bernard Gilpin, who was born at Kentmere Hall in 1517 and eventually became Archdeacon of Durham Cathedral. From Kentmere you can continue to explore the head of the valley on foot, or take footpaths 'over the top' into either the Troutbeck valley or the remote upper reaches of Longsleddale. Be warned, you need to arrive early in the village to find a parking space at busy times.

Kentmere Hall (a working farm and not open to the public) incorporates a 14th-century pele tower; this stout and uncompromisingly square defence was built to counter the constant threat of cross-border raids by the Scottish reivers.

THE APOSTLE OF THE NORTH

Bernard Gilpin, born at Kentmere Hall, became Archdeacon of Durham Cathedral and a leader of the Reformation; he was also known as 'The Apostle of the North'. When travelling to London in 1558 to face charges of heresy (the result of his attacks on the Roman Catholic Church), he fell and broke his leg. This turned out to be a 'lucky break' because while he was recovering Catholic Queen Mary died and her successor, Protestant Queen Elizabeth, restored him to favour, thus saving him from being burnt at the stake.

Remote moorland tops reflected in the still waters of Kentmere Tarn

Arni's Headland

Today Arnside, south of the Kent Channel, is well known to walkers because of the scenery and to birdwatchers because so many seabirds are attracted to the estuary. This is not a difficult walk and it provides some lovely views, but it includes a clifftop path that has some narrow stretches, so be sure to have suitable footwear.

Time: 3 hours. Distance: 5 miles (8km).
Location: Arnside, 10 miles (16km) south of Kendal on the south side of the Kent Channel, on the B5782, 4 miles (6.4km) off the A6.
Start: From the Albion pub at Arnside. Parking is available on the seafront. (OS grid ref: SD456788.)
OS Map: Outdoor Leisure 7 (English Lakes – South Eastern area) 1:25,000.
See Key to Walks on page 121.

ROUTE DIRECTIONS

From the Albion pub on the B5782 in **Arnside**, walk up the hill towards **Arnside Knott** and away from the seafront. At the top of the hill turn right into Redhills Road, and where High Knott Road leads uphill on the left, go through the gate and take the footpath that continues along the right-hand side of Dobshall Wood.

Stay on the path, passing bungalows, to reach a road, then keep left on the minor road, uphill, passing the Grange apartments. Keep on uphill along the track to the National Trust car park where you bear left, slightly uphill. Shortly, go through a gate in a wall and through woodland and another gate. Keep straight ahead on the path until you reach a junction of four paths.

Go through a gate on your right, waymarked 'Heathwaite', and continue downhill. From here there are fine views across **Morecambe Bay** and the sands to Morecambe. At the bottom of the field go through the gate to Hollins Farm. Cross the stile on the right, then proceed through the field keeping to the path for Far Arnside. Go through a stile in the far left-hand corner of the field, then turn right and continue along the road to Park Point.

The path goes through the caravan park (follow the fingerpost 'White Creek'). Turn left down the road with 'No entry' traffic signs and take the footpath leading into woodland. At a fork in the path by a tidal warning notice, take the left-hand fork down towards the coast. Take great care on the cliff path around Park Point and Arnside Point to White Creek, it is narrow in places and can be slippery in wet weather.

Nearing White Creek, pass through a gap in the wall on your left. Soon there are some caravans to your right, when you reach a stony track, turn up it to the right and through the caravan park, keeping to the main track until you reach New Barns. Turn right and

The view down the coast extends to the sweep of Morecambe Bay

follow the road back towards Arnside. From the shore the road rises round a double bend. Walk 1,000 yards (914m) into the village, then take the signed path on the left, opposite the post box. Continue downhill, then keep right at the shore to reach the promenade and the Albion.

POINTS OF INTEREST

Arnside

Arnside comes from the Norse personal name Arni and *saetr* (hill pasture). Although outside the Lake District National Park, together with Silverdale, Arnside has been designated an Area of Outstanding Natural Beauty and the views from the promenade show why. Situated at the mouth of the River Kent, it was once a busy port. The advent of the railway age in the mid 1800s made it an accessible resort. It is now a popular seaside village attracting weekend sailors and offering a variety of scenery, including limestone pavement, saltmarsh, foreshore fen, parkland and woodland.

Arnside Knott

There is a nature trail around Arnside Knott (522 feet/159m), which belongs to the National Trust and has numerous rare plants, unusual grasses and lovely trees. From the summit, on a fine day, a wide panorama is visible from the Pennines to the Lake District fells, notably the Old Man of Coniston, and across Morecambe Bay.

Morecambe Bay

Morecambe Bay has one of the fastest incoming tides in Britain which crosses a vast expanse of sand and mudflats. Unbelievably, there are 'rights of way' across these treacherous sands, and they can be crossed in the summer months with the aid of a guide who has detailed knowledge of the tides, quicksands and moving river channels. The Bay is well known to ornithologists, for over 200,000 wading birds and ducks (the largest estuary population in the country) feed on the mudflats.

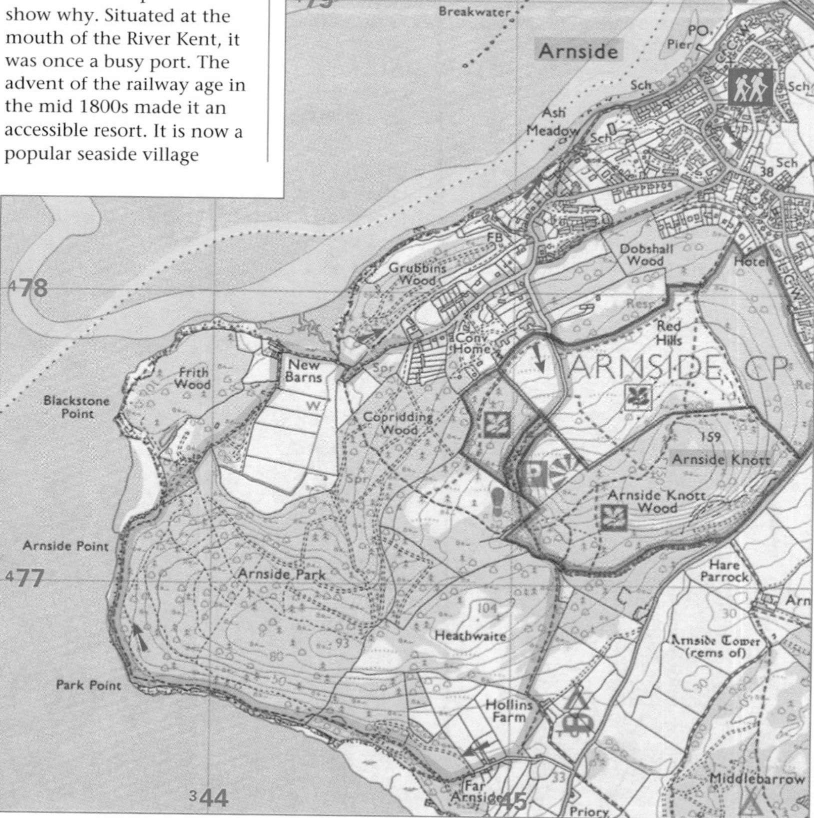

THE WATER POWER OF STICKLE TARN

A popular walk in the Great Langdale valley begins at the New Dungeon Ghyll Hotel, and passes the foaming white water of Dungeon Ghyll Force before finally climbing steeply uphill. A surprise awaits as you reach the top – the still waters of delectable Stickle Tarn, with the vertiginous cliff-face of Pavey Ark rearing up behind it.

Stickle Tarn is not quite as natural a lake as it first appears. A low dam was built to maintain a good head of water in the tarn, which was used to turn the waterwheel of a gunpowder mill in the valley bottom near Elter Water. Indeed, an old name for Stickle Ghyll was Mill Ghyll.

(Continued on page 29.)

KIRKSTONE PASS Map ref NY4008

As we change down a couple of gears and negotiate with ease some of Lakeland's most spectacular mountain passes, it is easy to forget what a challenge they represented to travellers of the past. For centuries the main way of transporting goods across the hills was by trains of packhorse ponies, each horse laden with a pair of pannier bags. Packhorse routes were created over some of the most forbidding landscapes in the Lake District; some were eventually upgraded into metalled roads, others are visited only by hiking boots.

Kirkstone Pass is, at a maximum of 1,489 feet (454m), the highest road in the Lake District, as well as one of the most spectacular. Charabancs used to labour up the long haul, from either Ambleside or Troutbeck; the Kirkstone Inn, where these roads converge, would have been a welcome sight for passengers. The pub, one of the most isolated in Cumbria, is still a popular halt; it takes its name from the nearby Kirk Stone, which resembles a church steeple.

The Kirkstone Pass continues through some magnificent mountain scenery, before dropping down, past Brothers Water, into Patterdale.

THE LANGDALES Map ref NY3006/3103

The Langdales are considered to be two of the most beautiful valleys in the Lake District. They are no big secret, as you will find if you try to make the circular drive around Great Langdale and Little Langdale on a weekend in high summer. The road is very narrow; better to leave your car at Skelwith Bridge or the village of Elterwater, and then tackle the delectable mountain scenery on foot. There are climbs and scrambles here to challenge the sure-footed, as well as lowland rambles for

An early morning mist lends an enchanted air to Little Langdale

those who just want to enjoy the view.

At Skelwith Bridge, where the B5343 Langdale road branches off from the A593, is Skelwith Force, where the River Brathay hammers over the rocks. Near by are the works of the Kirkstone Greenslate Quarries Company and their showrooms, the Kirkstone Galleries; the distinctive Lakeland slate has been quarried in this area for centuries. The path to the waterfall continues to Elter Water, where you can enjoy one of the views that seems to typify the Lake District – the distinctive silhouette of the Langdale Pikes. The twin humps of Harrison Stickle (2,415 feet/736m) and Pike of Stickle (2,323 feet/708m) are glimpsed from so many different vantage points. Those who know the Lake District well will recognise them from their outline alone.

Beyond the village of Chapel Stile, the Great Langdale valley opens up in spectacular fashion. The valley floor is divided up by stone walls, dotted with farmsteads and backed, on all sides, by a frieze of mountain peaks – a stunning landscape. The valley road meanders past the Old Dungeon Ghyll Hotel (this is where the Ambleside buses turn around). After a steep climb the road drops down, with views of Blea Tarn, into the Little Langdale valley. Though not as spectacular as the main valley, it is delightful and well supplied with good footpaths (see Walk on page 30). It is from Little Langdale that a minor road branches off, heading west, to become first Wrynose Pass and then Hardknott Pass, exciting driving for those whose brakes are in good order!

(Continued from page 28.)

Many mountain streams and becks in the Lake District were harnessed to power local mills and industries. Mills and their waterwheels can still be seen in Ambleside and Eskdale. Stott Park Bobbin Mill, near Newby Bridge (see page 21), is an example of a workshop that relied on water power to run its machines.

The Langdale Pikes have proved a popular subject with landscape painters over the years

A Blue Mountain Lake – Blea Tarn

A walk full of contrasts, combining areas of heather moorland with stunning views of the Langdale Pikes, Bow Fell, Crinkle Crags and Wetherlam. It includes a stroll around Blea Tarn and a stiff climb to the summit of Brown Howe. Boots with a good gripping sole are strongly recommended for this walk.

Time: 2½ hours. Distance: 3 miles (4.8km).
Location: Blea Tarn is situated on the unclassified road that links the valleys of Great Langdale and Little Langdale, 6 miles (9.7km) west of Ambleside, off the A593.
Start: At the National Trust car park near Blea Tarn. (OS grid ref: NY296043.)
OS Map: Outdoor Leisure 6 (The English Lakes – South Western Area) 1:25,000.
See Key to Walks on page 121.

ROUTE DIRECTIONS

Leave the car park and turn right along the road towards Bleatarn House. In front of you are the **Langdale Pikes** and Loft Crag. Thorn Crag can be seen in between Pike of Stickle (2,323 feet/708m) and Harrison Stickle (2,415 feet/736m). Approximately 110 yards (101m) before Bleatarn House, where the road bears downhill, turn sharp right on to an indistinct grass track that will take you up to a small ravine. Continue uphill on the track, with the ravine on your left, and through a wall on to a bracken-covered slope.

The path now meanders between small clumps of rocks, with occasional cairns indicating the route, which generally inclines slightly towards the right. Bear left just before you reach a wall and cross the bed at the top of the ravine near a group of larch trees. Cross the wall at the fenced gap, then bear left keeping parallel with a wall, passing several cairns, and continue to the summit of Brown Howe. To the north and east you have excellent panoramas of **Great Langdale**.

From the summit walk northwest along the crest, keeping the wall to your left. Beyond the tableland on your right is Lingmoor Tarn and as *ling* is the Scandinavian word for heather, we can be sure that it has been here for some time. It is well worth making a short diversion here (if you have time) to explore the area around the tarn, where there is a wealth of interesting flora and fauna.

Keeping on the main track, at the point where the wall changes to a fence and makes a right-angled turn downhill, keep ahad over a small 'top'. After taking a break to admire the views of the Langdale Pikes, continue ahead and follow the track as it veers back towards the wall. Continue next to the wall, and after some step-stones, go carefully down to a stile on the left. Climb over the stile and maintain this direction with the wall now on your right.

Once below Side Pike, turn left downhill, keeping the fence on your right all the way to the road. Turn right along the road, cross a cattle grid and turn immediately left to join a path (fence on your

Drystone walls, so much a part of the Lakeland scene, require careful maintenance

left) leading to the western corner of **Blea Tarn**. A gate leads into a wood of conifers and rhododendrons. On emerging from the wood, turn left over a footbridge and through another gate. The path will now take you directly to the road and car park.

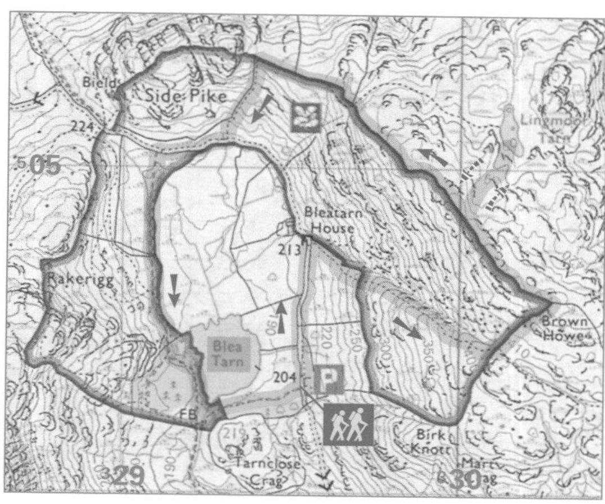

POINTS OF INTEREST

The Langdale Pikes

Looming high above Great Langdale are the most beautiful and much admired fells in the Lake District. The distinctive shapes of Harrison Stickle (2,415 feet/736m) and Pike of Stickle (2,323 feet/708m) have long been familiar with climbers, fell walkers, artists and photographers alike, making this area a most popular destination at any time of the year. On the slopes of Pike of Stickle is an 'axe factory', over 4,000 years old, where rock for axe heads was quarried and taken down to the valley for finishing.

The rushing waters of Stickle Ghyll, below the Pikes, are a further attraction amid this spectacular landscape.

Great Langdale and Little Langdale

Because of their isolation and their access to the sea, both these valleys were once used by smugglers. One legendary smuggler, Lanty Slee, kept his distilleries and rooms for storing illicit spirit at Fell Foot Farm at the end of the valley of Little Langdale.

Blea Tarn

Beautifully sited in a lofty position beneath Wrynose Fell, Blea Tarn is bordered by plantations of mixed trees and rhododendrons, making this a small oasis of civilisation in an otherwise wild place.

The striking view looking across Blea Tarn to Side Pike and Lingmoor

LEVENS HALL Map ref SD4984

Levens Hall, just off the junction of the A590 and the A6 south of Kendal, is well worth a visit. The beginnings of the Hall can be traced back to a 14th-century pele tower. Typically square, with thick walls and the narrowest of windows, the towers allowed the wealthier landowners to protect their families, livestock and servants in times of danger. The grim medieval tower at Levens was incorporated into a more elaborate Elizabethan building to create a comfortable family home. Levens Hall has passed through many hands, and now belongs to the Bagot family.

As fine as the house is, the most famous feature is outdoors. In 1688 Levens came into the possession of Colonel James Graham, who had a passion for gardening. He engaged Monsieur Beaumont to 'improve' on nature by creating a topiary garden, in which yew trees were clipped into a variety of shapes – resembling nothing so much as a surreal set of chess pieces. Such was the fame of the topiary gardens that people came from miles around, enduring bumpy coach rides to marvel at them. The designs we see today, probably the finest examples in the country, are much as they were designed three centuries ago.

Just a mile (1.6km) north of Levens Hall is Sizergh Castle, home of the Strickland family since 1239 and now in the custody of the National Trust. This is another building whose nucleus was a defensive pele tower that dates from the Scottish incursions of the 14th century.

THE GREY LADY'S CURSE

Levens Hall has more than its share of ghosts. One is the Grey Lady, able to walk straight through walls, and supposed to be the ghost of a gypsy woman who was refused refreshment at the Hall. She put a curse on the house, saying that no male heir would inherit Levens Hall until the River Kent ceased to flow and a white deer was seen in the park. The Hall did indeed pass through the female line until the birth of Alan Desmond Bagot in 1896 – an event that coincided with the river freezing over and the appearance of a white fawn.

LAKELAND WILDLIFE OASIS

At Hale, south of Milnthorpe, working models, 'hands-on' exhibits, computer programmes and a range of live animals demonstrate the evolution of life on earth. There are free-flying butterflies, exotic vegetation in the tropical houses, fish, reptiles, birds and mammals and a gift shop and café.

Magnificent yew topiary marks out the formal gardens at Levens Hall

Much altered in the intervening centuries, the house boasts fine oak panelling, intricately carved chimney mantels and a collection of family portraits. The gardens, with lovely views out over the lower Lakeland fells, are well worth exploring.

NEAR SAWREY Map ref SD3795
If the name of this tiny village isn't immediately familiar, you couldn't say the same about its most illustrious inhabitant. Beatrix Potter first came here on holiday in 1896, fell in love with the place and used the royalties from her first book, *The Tale of Peter Rabbit* (1901), to buy Hill Top. It was in this unpretentious little 17th-century farmhouse that she wrote many of the books that have delighted readers young and old throughout the world.

The success of the books allowed Beatrix Potter to buy up farms and land and all her properties were bequeathed, on her death in 1943, to the National Trust. Her will decreed that Hill Top should remain exactly as she had known it. Visitors will recognise specific details from the pictures in her books and even the adjacent inn, the Tower Bank Arms (also in the hands of the National Trust), will be familiar to readers of *The Tale of Jemima Puddleduck* (1908). Disregard its unprepossessing rendered exterior; Hill Top is chock full of Beatrix Potter memorabilia, including original drawings.

Hill Top is so popular that it is best avoided at peak holiday times. The Beatrix Potter Gallery at Hawkshead and The World of Beatrix Potter at Bowness hold a wealth of interst for 'Potterphiles'.

The grounds of Sizergh Castle boast fine gardens, including an extensive rock garden

THE NATIONAL PARK
The National Park Authority's main aims are to promote conservation, public enjoyment and the well-being of the local community. The biggest landowner within the Lake District National Park is the National Trust, which looks after large tracts of some of the finest Lakeland landscapes for the enjoyment of future generations. The Forestry Commission is another major landowner. North West Water, too, owns three large areas within the National Park, which include Haweswater, Thirlmere and Ennerdale. Most of the land is, however, in the hands of individual farmers and estates.

While the Wordsworths never actually owned Rydal Mount, William made the garden his own

DOROTHY WORDSWORTH
Dorothy Wordsworth's own literary reputation has suffered from standing in the huge shadow of her brother's poetic genius. Wordsworth himself knew better: 'She gave me eyes She gave me ears', he wrote. While Dorothy dedicated herself to domestic duties and acting as his amanuensis (she wrote the poems down as he dictated them), her own carefully observed prose has largely been overlooked. Yet it displays a simple joy in her Lakeland surroundings, and offers an intriguing counterpoint to William's more openly philosophical work.

RYDAL MOUNT Map ref NY3606
William Wordsworth had already written most of the poems on which his considerable reputation now rests by the time he and his family moved to Rydal Mount, their home until the poet's death in 1850. Still occupied by members of the Wordsworth family, the house, with its mementoes of a life devoted to literature, is open to the public and is featured on our Walk on page 18.

While living here, Wordsworth became Distributor of Stamps for Westmorland. More propitiously he accepted the honour of becoming Poet Laureate at the age of 73, on condition that he would not be required to compose verse on demand.

In the gardens, designed by Wordsworth himself, are the terrace and shelter where many of his later poems were composed. If you visit on a spring day you will find nearby Dora's Field (bought for, and named after, the poet's daughter) awash with wild daffodils. Even those who cannot recall another line of his poetry will know about the 'host of golden daffodils', though the genesis of the poem was actually a walk that his sister Dorothy took along the shores of Ullswater.

TROUTBECK Map ref NY4002
With its houses spread out along narrow country lanes, without any recognisable centre, Troutbeck hardly qualifies as a village. The groupings are based around a

number of wells and springs which, until recent times, were the only source of drinking water. However, lovers of vernacular architecture will find a collection of buildings, dating from the 16th to the 19th centuries, that retain original features such as mullioned windows, heavy cylindrical chimneys and a now rare example of an exposed spinning gallery. Troutbeck is now designated a Conservation Area.

The best-preserved (if not the oldest) building in the Troutbeck valley is Townend, a fine example of a yeoman farmer's house. Built by George Browne in 1626, it was still the home of his descendants in 1943, and was bought by the National Trust soon after that. Townend offers a fascinating glimpse into what domestic life was like for Lakeland's wealthier farmers, with low ceilings, original home-carved oak panelling and furniture and stone-flagged floors.

ULVERSTON Map ref SD2878

Ulverston, on the fringe of Morecambe Bay, is sufficiently off the beaten track to maintain an unhurried air, though Thursdays and Saturdays find the market square thronged with stalls. On top of Hoad Hill, overlooking the town and a landmark for miles around, is a 90-foot (27.4m) copy of the Eddystone Lighthouse. It is no help to ships, however, being a monument to Sir John Barrow, Ulverston-born in 1764. A founder member of the Royal Geographical Society, his story is told in the town's heritage centre.

In Upper Brook Street the Laurel and Hardy Museum is a mecca for those who can't hear the Cuckoo Waltz without thinking of the bowler-hatted buffoons of the silver screen. It is not so much a museum as a

ROMAN ROAD

The Troutbeck valley offers one way of reaching the spectacular Kirkstone Pass (the other route is via Ambleside). The Romans used the valley as the starting point for a remarkable road, High Street, which took a typically uncompromising route straight across the mountain ridges that lie between the lakes of Ullswater and Haweswater.

The road is believed to have been built to link the Roman forts at Ambleside and Brougham with their port at Ravenglass on the west coast.

Swarthmoor Hall, Ulverston became the home of Quaker leader George Fox when he married widow Mary Fell

ULVERSTON'S CANAL

Ulverston has the shortest canal in the country, just a mile (1.6km) long, that links the town to the sea. Built by engineer John Rennie in 1794, it represents the high point of Ulverston's iron-ore industry; near by were the town's foundry and blast furnace. Ships could navigate into the town to be loaded with cargoes of iron and slate. The canal had a working life of 50 years, after which it was made redundant by the coming of the railway. Ulverston went into decline as the iron-ore industry gradually moved to Barrow. Today the canal towpath (you can find the canal basin behind the Canal Tavern on the A590) provides a pleasant walk down to the sea.

haphazard collection of Laurel and Hardy memorabilia, assembled here because Stan Laurel, the thin one, was born in Ulverston in 1890. No souvenir is deemed too trivial for inclusion in the displays, so visitors can admire, for example, an otherwise unremarkable set of curtains from Stan Laurel's home in Beverly Hills. Visitors can watch clips from some of the pair's 105 films in a tiny cinema shoehorned into a corner of the museum.

WINDERMERE AND BOWNESS-ON-WINDERMERE

Map ref SD4198/4097

To many visitors, a visit to 'the Lakes' implies nothing more strenuous than mooching around the shops of Windermere and Bowness, and a relaxing boat trip on the lake. It cannot be denied that these twin towns (almost joined into one these days) attract a disproportionate number of holiday-makers; those in search of the National Park's ethos, 'quiet recreation', should look elsewhere. Though traffic congestion is a perennial problem around the area, walkers can escape the crowds surprisingly quickly – even on the busiest of Bank Holidays.

The popularity of Windermere and Bowness is largely historical. Windermere is as far into the heart of the Lake District as the railway was ever driven. William Wordsworth lamented the coming of the railway; he foresaw that his beloved Lakeland would be spoiled irretrievably by an influx of visitors. Certainly the railway opened up the Lakeland landscape to working

A host of golden tulips dance in the breeze at Waterhead, on lake Windermere

Wooden launches of a bygone era share moorings with more modern craft at the lakeside

people, instead of just the well-heeled travellers with time on their hands. Wordsworth was right, of course – the Lake District has changed dramatically. On the other hand, millions of people are now able to enjoy the unrivalled scenery. This, in a nutshell, is the one big quandary faced by the National Park Authority.

It may seem odd that it is Windermere, rather than Bowness at the water's edge, that takes its name from the lake. This was simply to provide the railway station with a more appealing name; until the opening of the branch line in 1847, Windermere was known as Birthwaite.

Bowness takes the hordes of visitors in a warm embrace, continually discovering new enterprises. A few years ago it was hard to find a decent place to eat; now you can take your pick from a wide array of eateries, including cafés, bistros, pizza parlours, Indian restaurants and the ever-popular fish and chip take-aways.

The water of England's longest lake laps gently on the beach at Bowness Bay. Swans and ducks, fed by visitors, enjoy an indolent lifestyle. Sleek clinker-built dinghies can be hired by the hour. The less energetic can enjoy a lake-long cruise, via Waterhead and Lakeside (linking to the steam trains of the restored Lakeside–Haverthwaite Railway), on the cruise ships *Tern, Teal* and *Swan*. *Tern,* with sleek lines and upturned prow, is more than a hundred years old and was once steam-powered. From 2005 Windermere will become a more peaceful lake when the National Park Authority's hotly contested 10mph water speed limit takes effect.

Directly opposite Bowness Bay is Belle Isle. In 1774, when notions of the 'romantic' and 'picturesque' were at their height, a Mr English built an eccentric residence. Its

LAKELAND CHAR

Originally an Arctic fish, the char thrives in the cool depths of Windermere. It has long been considered a delicacy, and visitors would be sure to take some potted char home with them. The fish is still served in many Lakeland hotels. This demand is satisfied by char fishermen who row their dinghies up and down the lake, patiently trailing weighted lines baited with spinners, to tempt the deep-water char.

A well-used tea kettle is polished to perfection on board an exhibit at the Windermere Steamboat Museum

round design brought so much ridicule on his head (William Wordsworth, for example, called it 'a pepperpot') that Mr English was prompted to sell his unusual home.

The island site was earlier occupied by a manor house which was besieged by Roundheads while the Royalist owner was busy fighting other battles in Carlisle (see side panel on page 23). Archaeological finds reveal Belle Isle was occupied during Roman times. It was bought in 1781 as a present for Mrs Isabella Curwen, and renamed in the lady's honour. While most of Windermere's little islands are now in the hands of the National Trust, beautiful Belle Isle is still privately owned.

At the bottom of Bowness Hill, a couple of minutes' walk from the lake, is The Old Laundry, which caters for visitors and locals alike. As well as a theatre, there is a regular programme of exhibitions and events. Here, too, you will find the World of Beatrix Potter, which uses the latest technology to bring to life the stories of Peter Rabbit, Jemima Puddleduck and the other characters that have delighted many generations of children. Thanks to animatronics, some of these familiar figures are capable of life-like movements.

At the Windermere Steamboat Museum, on the A592 Bowness to Ambleside road, you will find a fascinating collection of craft; mostly steam-powered launches from the Victorian and Edwardian eras when each new craft seemed to be more elegant than the last. Fortunately, a large number have been saved from an ignominious fate. They are moored afloat in a wet dock and some are taken out on to Windermere; their peaceful progress across the water is in sharp contrast to the cacophony of the modern speedboats.

Here, happily restored, is *Esperance*, the conveyance of shipping magnate Henry William Schneider when he travelled to his office in Barrow. The steam launch *Dolly*, built in 1850, is acknowledged to be the oldest boat in the world to be mechanically propelled. Lovers of Arthur Ransome's children's books, such as *Swallows and Amazons*, will be happy to find the author's own rowing boat on display.

HOLEHIRD GARDENS

On the A592, ¾ mile (1.2km) north of its junction with the A591, are Holehird Gardens, the Lakeland Horticultural Society gardens. They are unmatched in Cumbria and give glorious views towards the central fells.

THE FERRY

A car ferry crosses Windermere between Ferry Nab and Ferry House, just to the south of Bowness, saving motorists a long drive around the lake. On summer weekends, however, it might take just as long to wait in a queue for the ferry. Markings on the approach indicate how long you might have to wait. But what's the hurry? An earlier version of the Windermere ferry was used by William Wordsworth (like him, you never need to wait more than a few minutes if you arrive on foot).

A further 2½ miles (4km) north along the Ambleside road brings you to Brockhole, a fine house set in delightful gardens that shelve down to the lake shore. Built for a prominent Manchester businessman, the house has, since the late 1960s, been the National Park Visitor Centre. Here visitors can learn just why the Lake District is so special, and why every effort should be made to preserve the landscape for future generations to enjoy. Brockhole is an excellent first stop for visitors new to the Lake District. There are gardens, displays, exhibitions, an adventure playground and a calendar of special events.

The eastern shore of Windermere is, for much of its length, in private hands. Mill owners who prospered from the trade in wool and cotton eagerly bought up plots of land to create tranquil oases with views of the lake. Thus it is that the drive along the lake (on the A592) can be disappointing; there are few public access points where people can enjoy a stroll by the water's edge. The less-populated western shore, much of it in the stewardship of the National Trust, offers delightful lake-side walking.

For an elevated view of the lake, take a path to the left of the Windermere Hotel (at the top of the town). Within a few minutes you will be able to enjoy a glorious view of the lake and the southern Lakeland fells from the vantage point of Orrest Head. Another excellent viewpoint is the rounded hill called Gummer's How, which can be approached via a minor road just north of Newby Bridge. From the top (half an hour's walk from the car park) you will be able to see almost the length of Windermere, making the yachts and motor boats seem like tiny toys.

THINGS TO DO

A list of events at Brockhole and throughout the National Park is available from the address on page 40 or tel: 015394 46601.

BLACKWELL

This superb Arts and Crafts country house, a Grade 1 Listed building, overlooks Windermere from the B5360 1½ miles (2.4km) south of Bowness. It opened in 2001 as and international crafts venue.

The Lake District Visitor Centre at Brockhole, on the lake between Windermere and Ambleside

Kendal, Windermere and the Kent Estuary

Checklist

Leisure Information
Places of Interest
Shopping
The Performing Arts
Sports, Activities and the Outdoors
Annual Events and Customs

Leisure Information

TOURIST INFORMATION CENTRES

Ambleside
Central Buildings, Market Cross. Tel: 015394 32582.

Brockhole
On the A591 between Windermere and Ambleside. Tel: 015394 46601.

Bowness-on-Windermere
Glebe Road, Bowness Bay. Tel: 015394 42895.

Coniston
Main car park. Tel: 015394 41533.

Grange-over-Sands
Victoria Hall, Main Street. Tel: 015395 34026.

Grasmere
Red Bank Road. Tel: 015394 35245.

Hawkshead
Main Car Park. Tel: 015394 36525 (seasonal).

Kendal
Town Hall, Highgate. Tel: 01539 725758.

Kirkby Lonsdale
24 Main Street. Tel: 015242 71437.

Sedbergh
Main Street. Tel: 015396 20125.

Ulverston
Coronation Hall, County Square. Tel: 01229 587120.

Waterhead
Ambleside. Tel: 015394 32729.

Windermere
Victoria Street. Tel: 015394 46499.

LAKE DISTRICT NATIONAL PARK INFORMATION POINTS

Elterwater
Maple Tree Corner Shop.

Far Sawrey
The Post Office.

Rusland
Forest Spinners.

OTHER INFORMATION

Cumbria Wildlife Trust
Brockhole, Windermere. Tel: 015394 48280.

English Heritage
Canada House, 3 Chepstow St, Manchester. Tel: 0161 242 1400 www.english-heritage.org.uk

Forestry Commission
Grizedale Forest Visitor Centre, Grizedale, Hawkshead, Ambleside. Tel: 01229 860010.

Lake District National Park Authority Headquarters
Murley Moss, Oxenholme Road, Kendal. Tel: 01539 724555. www.lake-district.gov.uk

National Trust in Cumbria
The Hollens, Grasmere, Ambleside, Cumbria. Tel: 015394 35599. www.nationaltrust.org.uk

Parking
Information on parking permits and car parks in the area is available from local Tourist Information Centres.

Public Transport
The Traveline service gives details of buses, boats, trains and ferries operating throughout Cumbria. Tel: 0870 608 2608.

Weather
Lake District Weather Service. Tel: 017687 75757.

ORDNANCE SURVEY MAPS

Landranger 1:50,000
Sheets 96, 97.
Outdoor Leisure 1:25,000
Sheets 6, 7.

Places of Interest

There will be an admission charge at the following places of interest unless otherwise stated.

Abbot Hall Art Gallery
Kirkland, Kendal. Tel: 01539 722464. One of Britain's finest small galleries. Open mid-Feb to late Dec, daily.

Abbot Hall Museum of Lakeland Life and Industry
Kirkland, Kendal. Tel: 01539 722464. Open mid-Feb to late Dec, daily.

Ambleside Museum
Rydal Road. Tel: 015394 312312. Open daily.

Beatrix Potter Gallery
Main Street, Hawkshead. Tel: 015394 36355. Open Apr–Oct, most days.

Blackwell
Bowness. Tel: 015394 46139. Open all year, daily, except Christmas to end Jan.

Brantwood
Coniston. Tel: 015394 41396. Open mid-Mar to mid-Nov daily; rest of year, certain days.

Cartmel Priory
Cartmel, Grange-over-Sands. Tel: 015395 36261. Open all year, daily. Free.

Dove Cottage and The Wordsworth Museum
Grasmere. Tel: 015394 35544/35547. The poet's home from 1799 to 1808. Open all year daily, except early Jan to early Feb and Christmas.

Hill Top
Near Sawrey. Tel: 015394 36269. Open Apr–Oct, certain days.

Holker Hall and Gardens
Cark-in-Cartmel, Grange-over-Sands. Tel: 015395 58328. Includes the Lakeland Motor Museum. Open Apr–Oct, most days.

Kendal Museum of Natural History and Archaeology
Station Road, Kendal. Tel: 01539 721374. Open mid-Feb to Dec, most days.

Lake District Visitor Centre at Brockhole
Windermere. Tel: 015394 46601. Open early Apr–early Nov, daily; grounds and gardens open all year, daily.

Laurel and Hardy Museum
4c Upper Brook Street, Ulverston. Tel: 01229 582292. Open Feb–Dec, daily, except Christmas Day.

Levens Hall
Kendal. Fine house and magnificent yew topiary gardens. Tel: 015395 60321. Open Apr–Oct, certain days.

Quaker Tapestry Exhibition Centre
New Road, Kendal. Tel: 01539 722975. Open Apr–Dec, most days.

Ruskin Museum
The Institute, Coniston. Tel: 015394 41164. Open Easter to mid-Nov, daily.

Rydal Mount
Rydal. Tel: 01539 433002. Open Mar–Oct daily; Nov-Feb most days; closed last two weeks Jan.

Sizergh Castle
Sizergh, near Kendal. Tel: 015395 60070. Open early Apr–Oct, most afternoons.

Stott Park Bobbin Mill
near Newby Bridge. Tel: 015395 31087. Open Apr–Oct, daily.

Swarthmoor Hall
Ulverston. Tel: 01229 583204. Open Mar–Oct, some afternoons.

Townend
Troutbeck, Windermere. Tel: 015394 32628. Open early Apr–Oct, most afternoons.

Windermere Steamboat Museum
Rayrigg Road, Windermere. Tel: 015394 45565. Open late Mar–Oct, daily. Steam boats subject to availability and weather.

The World of Beatrix Potter
The Old Laundry, Bowness-on-Windermere. Tel: 015394 88444. Open all year daily except Christmas and late Jan.

SPECIAL INTEREST FOR CHILDREN

The following places may be of interest to visitors with children. Unless otherwise stated, there will be an admission charge.

The Aquarium of the Lakes
Lakeside, Newby Bridge. Tel: 015395 30153. Open daily, except Christmas Day.

Lakeland Wildlife Oasis
Milnthorpe, near Kendal. Tel: 015395 63027. Open daily, except 25, 26 Dec.

Lakeside and Haverthwaite Railway
Lakeside, Newby Bridge. Tel: 015395 31594. Open daily, Easter and May–Oct.

Windermere Steamboat Museum
Rayrigg Road, Windermere. Tel: 015394 45565. Open late Mar–Oct, daily. Steam boats subject to availability and weather.

The World of Beatrix Potter
The Old Laundry, Bowness-on-Windermere. Tel: 015394 88444. Open all year daily except Christmas and late Jan.

Shopping

Ambleside
Market, Wed.

Kendal
Market, Wed, Sat. 'K' Village Factory Shopping Centre.

Ulverston
Market, Thu, Sat.

LOCAL SPECIALITIES

Char
Available in Windermere.

Crafts
The *Made in Cumbria* guide to workshops and galleries is available from Tourist Information Centres. Their web site lists over 400 members (craftspeople and artists) who

Brantwood, on the wooded slope above Coniston Water, was the home of John Ruskin

produce everything from gifts to furniture and speciality foods, all made in Cumbria.
www.madeincumbria.co.uk

Cumberland Sausages
Available from local butchers and markets.

Gingerbread
The Gingerbread Shop, Grasmere. Tel: 015394 35428.

Herdwick Lamb
Available from local butchers and markets.

Kendal Mint Cake
Available throughout Cumbria.

Mills
Heron Corn Mill, Beetham, Milnthorpe. Tel: 015395 65027. Open Apr–Sep. Gleaston Water Mill, Ulverston. Tel: 01229 869244.

Morecambe Bay Shrimps
Available from local fishmongers.

The Performing Arts

The Brewery Arts Centre
Kendal. Tel: 01539 725133.

The Old Laundry
Crag Brow, Bowness-on-Windermere. Tel: 015394 88444.

Coronation Hall
Ulverston. Tel: 01229 582610.

Sports, Activities and the Outdoors

ANGLING

Freshwater
Numerous oportunities for fishing on farms, lakes and rivers. Permits and licences are available from local tackle shops and Tourist Information Centres.

BOAT TRIPS

Coniston
Coniston Ferry Services, Castle Buildings, Near Sawrey, Ambleside. Tel: 015394 36216. Steam Yacht *Gondola*, Pier Cottage, Coniston. Tel: 015394 63856.

Windermere
Windermere Lake Cruises, Lakeside, Newby Bridge, Ulverston. Tel: 015395 31188 or 015394 43360. Windermere Steamboat Museum, Rayrigg Road. Tel: 015394 45565.

COUNTRY PARKS, FORESTS NATURE RESERVES

Grizedale Forest Park, Grizedale. Tel: 01229 860010.
www.grizedaleforestpark.co.uk

CYCLE HIRE

Ambleside
Biketreks, Compston Road. Tel: 015394 31505.

Coniston
Summitreks, 14 Yewdale Road. Tel: 015394 41212.

Staveley
Millennium Cycles, Crook Road. Tel: 01539 821167.

Windermere
Country Lanes, Windermere Railway Station. Tel: 015394 44544.

GOLF COURSES

Grange-over-Sands
Grange Fell Golf Club, Fell Road. Tel: 015395 32536.
Grange-over-Sands Golf Club, Meathop Road. Tel: 015395 33180/33754.

Kendal
Kendal Golf Club, The Heights. Tel: 01539 724079/733708.

Kirkby Lonsdale
Kirkby Lonsdale Golf Club, Barbon. Tel: 015242 76365.

Ulverston
Ulverston Golf Club, Bardsea. Tel: 01229 582824.

Windermere
Windermere Golf Club, Cleabarrow. Tel: 015394 43123.

GOLF DRIVING RANGES

Kendal
Kendal Golf Driving Range, Oxenholme Farm, Oxenholme Road. Tel: 01539 733933.

HORSE-RIDING

Kendal
Holmescales Riding Centre, Holmescales Farm, Old Hutton. Tel: 01539 729388.

Windermere
Lakeland Equestrian, Wynlass Beck Stables, Wynlass Beck. Tel 015394 43811.

Annual Events and Customs

Ambleside
Rushbearing Ceremony, first Saturday in July.
Ambleside Sports, late July.
Lake District Summer Music Festival, early to mid-August.

Cartmel
Cartmel Steeplechases, Spring Bank Holiday.
Cartmel Agricultural Show, early August.
Cartmel Races, August Bank Holiday.

Coniston
Coniston Water Festival, late May to early June.

Grange-over-Sands
Edwardian Festival, mid-June.
Lakeland Rose Show, mid-July.

Grasmere
Grasmere Gala, mid-June.
Rushbearing Ceremony, early August.
Grasmere Sports and Show, late August.

Kendal
Kendal Torchlight Procession, early September.
Westmorland County Show, early September.

Kirkby Lonsdale
Lunesdale Show, mid-August.
Victorian Fair, early September.

Rydal
Rydal Sheepdog Trials, mid-August.

Staveley
Lake District Sheepdog Trials, early August.

Ulverston
North Lonsdale Agricultural Show, late July.
Lantern Procession, mid-September.

These checklists give details of just some of the facilities within the area covered by this guide. Further information can be obtained from Tourist Information Centres.

Eskdale and Wasdale

The southern peninsulas of Cartmel and Furness attract fewer visitors than central Lakeland, not least because this area is excluded from so many maps of the Lake District! It is a little unfair. The delightful narrow-gauge Ravenglass and Eskdale Railway, which once transported iron-ore from the Eskdale mines to the coast, now steams along the valley of the River Esk carrying tourists and hikers alike, whilst unspoilt Dunnerdale is a haven for those wanting solitude amid delightful scenery. The coastal area – away from industrialised Barrow-in-Furness – offers much to walkers, birdwatchers and lovers of quiet places.

BARROW-IN-FURNESS Map ref SD2068

Even the most loyal of locals would hesitate to describe Barrow as beautiful. Until the mid-19th century there was just a tiny fishing village on the tip of the Furness peninsula. What made it grow at an astonishing rate were the iron- and steel-making industries, closely followed, logically, by the building of ships.

The shipbuilding company of Vickers became almost synonymous with Barrow, and even today, long after the great days of British shipbuilding have gone, the docks and shipyards are an impressive sight. For a fascinating overview of the industry, past and present, head for one of the town's most popular attractions, the Dock

WORDSWORTH AND THE FURNESS PENINSULA

The young William Wordsworth made a number of trips, on horseback, to the Furness peninsula. The red sandstone ruins of Furness Abbey inspired him to feature them in 'The Prelude' and a couple of sonnets. He knew Barrow-in-Furness too, but only as a small village as yet untouched by the ship-building industry that transformed the town so rapidly.

A decommissioned lifeboat stands guard outside Barrow's Dock Museum

THE CISTERCIAN WAY
The Cistercian Way is a 33-mile (52.8km) walk from Grange-over-Sands to Roa Island, near Barrow-in-Furness. The route explores the Cartmel and Furness peninsulas, visiting some interesting places on the way, including Cartmel Priory, Furness Abbey and Swarthmoor Hall, the 16th-century manor house that was once the home of George Fox, the founder of Quakerism.

Museum on North Road. Sitting astride a deep dry dock, the museum tells how, in the space of a generation, Barrow became a major force in maritime engineering. Other exhibits focus on older shipbuilding traditions, and the pioneers whose foresight and inventiveness helped Britain to lead the way.

A surprise awaits those who drive past the museum – a road-bridge links Barrow with the Isle of Walney. A cursory glance at the map shows this to be a geographic oddity shielding the tip of the Furness peninsula, and Barrow itself, from the ravages of the sea. The southern tip of the Isle of Walney is a haven for wildlife.

Between Barrow and Dalton, in the 'Vale of Deadly Nightshade', is Furness Abbey. Now an evocative ruin of weathered, salmon-coloured sandstone, it was, in its heyday, second only in importance to Fountains Abbey in North Yorkshire. Separated from the rest of England by sea and mountains, Furness Abbey achieved a remarkable degree of feudal independence, owning outlying farms, known as 'granges', as far afield as Lincolnshire and Ireland. Parts of the abbey (now in the hands of English Heritage) still stand to substantially their full height, in a romantic wooded setting. The towers, arches and windows rise up in an architectural embodiment of Christian faith; the size of the community can be estimated by the fact that the monks' dormitory is fully 200 feet (61m) long.

The nearby village of Dalton-in-Furness, now a quiet backwater, was once the capital of Furness and the main market town for the area; but that role has passed now to Ulverston. On one side of the old market square is Dalton Castle, an uncompromisingly square sandstone building that was built by the monks of Furness Abbey as a courthouse and prison.

Sturdy Norman arches support the remaining cloister walls at Furness Abbey

Duddon Bridge spans the river shallows

DUNNERDALE Map ref SD2195

Unlike those areas of the Lake District that have sold their soul to tourism, Dunnerdale is as delightful and unspoilt as it was when William Wordsworth first explored the valley. The River Duddon rises in the hills by the Wrynose Pass, and reaches the sea at its own estuary of Duddon Sands. In between are 10 miles (16km) of the most delectable scenery that you can find anywhere within the National Park – not the most dramatic, not the most spectacular, but those who love more intimate landscapes will find Dunnerdale a delight.

The handsome little town of Broughton-in-Furness stands back from the Duddon Estuary. The market square, dominated by a huge chestnut tree, boasts a stepped obelisk and a pair of stone tables that were once used to sell fish caught in the River Duddon.

From Duddon Bridge a minor road takes you up Dunnerdale. You are seldom far from the river which is rocky and fast flowing, and the natural habitat of dippers and wagtails. There are grassy riverbanks that seem designed for spreading out a picnic blanket. Ulpha, merely a straggle of houses and farmsteads, is the only village in the valley.

As you continue to climb, the fields and woods give way to a more rugged landscape, as Harter Fell 2,139 feet (652m) and the higher peaks of central Lakeland begin to dominate the view. When you reach a road junction, at Cockley Beck, your choice of road is between two of the most spectacular routes in the country, you can either travel west to Eskdale via the tortuous Hardknott Pass, or east, along Wrynose Pass, and down into the beautiful Little Langdale valley.

THE DUDDON VALLEY

William Wordsworth – who knew a thing or two about beautiful landscapes – was much taken with Dunnerdale. He knew it as the Duddon Valley, and enshrined it in a sequence of sonnets. Walkers who enjoy their own company, rather than hordes of fellow hikers, can follow in the poet's footsteps and enjoy the solitude and intimate landscape of Dunnerdale.

Bathed in sunshine, Eskdale Green lies toward the western end of this quiet valley

DRYSTONE WALLS

The landscape of the Lake District is divided by thousands of miles of drystone walls. Some of these walls are hundreds of years old, but most were constructed during the 18th and 19th centuries when the open fells were enclosed. They were built to withstand the extremes of the weather and the passing of time, and remain as monuments to the men who made them.

ESKDALE Map ref NY1701

Here is another beautiful valley that is relatively quiet when so many other places are chock-full of tourists. The reason is inaccessibility; to explore Eskdale most visitors have to negotiate the twists, turns and 1-in-3 (33%) hairpins of the Hardknott and Wrynose Passes, or else take the long way round, meandering through south Lakeland. All the better, then, for those who venture this far west, for Eskdale is well worth the effort.

This is excellent walking country, with plentiful rights of way and room to roam. For over 30 years the Ravenglass and Eskdale Railway has enabled hikers and sightseers to venture into the heart of Eskdale without blocking up the narrow road with their cars. This delightful narrow-gauge railway used to carry iron ore from the Eskdale mines to the coast; now the diminutive steam engines carry passengers up the valley. There are seven stations along the line, all offering excellent opportunities for scenic walks along with the option of taking a later train back down to Ravenglass.

The terminus, at Dalegarth, is just a short walk from Boot, a tiny village with a friendly pub, the Burnmoor Inn. Just up the valley, the Woolpack recalls a time when this was a watering hole for the men who drove packponies laden with fleeces down to the coast. Beyond a packhorse bridge spanning Whillan Beck is the delectable grouping of tiny buildings that comprise Eskdale Mill. Cereals have been ground here since 1578, but milling ended during the 1920s. The overshot waterwheel was adapted to supply electricity to upper Eskdale; the valley was connected to the mains in 1955.

GOSFORTH Map ref NY0603

Sandwiched between Wasdale and Sellafield – 'beauty and the beast', you could say – is the village of Gosforth. Vikings, settling in the area, were gradually converted to the Christian faith, and the sandstone church at Gosforth boasts a number of artefacts dating back to this period, more than 1,000 years ago. In the churchyard is a Viking cross which is 14 feet (4.3m) high and so slender that the wonder is that it has survived intact. Intricate carving on all four sides combines Viking legends with Christian teaching.

Another ancient cross in the churchyard was converted, in a fit of official vandalism two centuries ago, into a sundial. Other relics, now displayed inside the church, fared better: the Fishing Stone and a pair of hog-back tombstones are potent symbols of the coming together, many centuries ago, of two disparate cultures.

HARDKNOTT PASS AND ROMAN FORT

Map ref NY2301

When you gaze down from the remains of the fort at the western end of the Hardknott Pass (1,291 feet/393m) it is easy to see why the Romans chose this site. Hardknott Castle Roman Fort (known to the Romans as *Mediobogdum*, and now in the care of English Heritage) enjoys a commanding panorama down into the green valley of Eskdale. Attacks from three sides were impossible and a trench forestalled attacks from the east.

Soldiers were garrisoned here to safeguard the road they had constructed to link the fort at Ambleside and the port of Ravenglass. Preferring to take the most direct route whenever possible, they drove their road over the most difficult terrain through what we now know as the

THE CUMBRIA CYCLE WAY

The Cumbria Cycle Way runs in an almost circular route for 259 miles (414.4km) around the county border. It can be cycled in either direction, but experts suggest that clockwise is better, to take advantage of prevailing winds along the west coast section. Mostly it uses minor roads, with some sections on bridleways and former railway lines. A guide book is available from the Tourist Information Centres, listing seven stages of about 37 miles each (59.2km), all ending in places providing accommodation.

Looking north from Hardknott to Scafell

Hardknott and Wrynose Passes.

Despite the wonderful views, the Roman soldiers must have regarded isolated, windswept *Mediobogdum* as an unglamorous posting. The perimeter wall is of typical playing-card shape and the ruins are still impressive. The soldiers drilled on a flat parade ground near by. The bath house would have represented one of their few comforts.

Hardknott Pass, rising 1,000 feet (305m) out of Eskdale in little more than a mile (1.6km), is one of the most spectacular roads in the country; a few of the hairpin bends are as steep as 1-in-3 (33%). The ascent holds few terrors for car drivers these days; most problems arise at peak holiday times when too many people are making the trip. And if the road is icy, or you are towing a caravan, don't even consider it!

THE ROMAN FORT

An inscribed stone, originally over the main gate of the fort at Hardknott, records that it was built by a cohort from Dalmatia (part of the former Yugoslavia) for the 'Emperor Caesar Trajan Hadrian Augustus'. Pottery found here during the extensive excavations suggests that the fort was occupied between AD 120 and 197.

MILLOM Map ref SD1780

On its own peninsula overlooking the estuary of the River Duddon, Millom is well off the beaten track. The town grew with the iron and steel industries in the latter years of the 19th century. The Millom Folk Museum and the Tourist Information Centre are both housed in the imaginatively redeveloped railway station. The museum has vivid reminders of the town's iron-mining days, including a full scale reconstruction of an iron ore drift mine, as well as items associated with Norman Nicholson, Millom's own poet.

The Hodbarrow Iron Works, which closed in the 1960s, have been encouraged to 'go back to nature'. The result is a brackish lagoon, adjacent to the Duddon Estuary, which is now an RSPB reserve. This stretch of water acts as a magnet for breeding wildfowl, waders and the rare natterjack toad.

THE SWINSIDE STONE CIRCLE

The Swinside stone circle can be found on a spur of Black Combe, a little-explored fell, off the A596 between Millom and Broughton-in-Furness. Though lying on private land, the circle of 57 standing stones can be viewed from an adjacent right of way. The circle is similar in size to Castlerigg stone circle, near Keswick, though cannot boast a similarly spectacular setting.

The remains of Millom Castle, now part of a farm, date back to the 14th century

There's an old bridge by the stream at Muncaster Mill

MUNCASTER CASTLE Map ref SD1096

Few stately homes can boast a view to match the panorama from the terrace of Muncaster Castle. Directly below are gardens, featuring one of the largest collection of rhododendron species in the country. In the middle distance the River Esk meanders prettily through the lowlands. The horizon is taken up by a frieze of starkly delineated Lakeland peaks, of which Scafell Pike at 3,210 feet (978m) is the most prominent.

In 1208 the land at Muncaster was granted to the Pennington family, and is still in the family's ownership today. The sandstone castle is a major addition to a 14th-century pele tower, which was itself built on Roman foundations. Visitors get a 'guided tour' (on tape, at least) by the present owner, detailing the many treasures and artworks to be found.

Muncaster Castle is also the headquarters of the World Owl Trust, dedicated to worldwide owl conservation. Visitors can see a variety of owls, from the pygmy owl to the gigantic eagle owl, and from our own native species to some of the rarest owls in the world. On summer afternoons visitors get a chance to 'Meet the Birds' and, weather permitting, watch them in flight.

As Lords of the Manor, the Pennington family owned Muncaster Mill from the 15th century right up to 1961, when the mill closed. The present buildings, dating from about 1700, are easily reached by car on the A595 or by taking a ride on the Ravenglass and Eskdale Railway (the mill is a 'request halt' on the line). The tiny mill, with its overshot wheel turned by water from the River Mite, is a reminder of a time when every village boasted its own corn mill. Now restored to full working order, the mill grinds corn once again, and freshly milled products are on sale.

MUNCASTER'S CURIOSITIES

A couple of curiosities in Muncaster Castle are worthy of mention. A painting on the upstairs landing features a surprisingly glum-looking Thomas Skelton, the last Fool of Muncaster, whose antics and friendship with William Shakespeare gave rise to the word 'Tomfoolery'.

Another picture was painted by Thomas Gainsborough to settle a wager. He had been shown a pencil drawing of a picture by Titian, and was challenged to produce his own version in exactly the same colours as in Titian's original. He won his bet, and the picture – a group portrait – now hangs in the dining room.

The walls of the former bath house stand tall at Ravenglass, a tribute to Roman masonry skills

RAVENGLASS Map ref SD0896

The Roman fort and harbour of Ravenglass were known to the Romans as *Glannoventa*; up to 1,000 men were garrisoned here. Little remains of this settlement, just a short stroll to the south of the village, except for the ruins of a bath house. Rising to a maximum of 12 feet (3.7m), these are probably the highest extant Roman ruins in the country.

Ravenglass today comprises a short street of houses which ends abruptly at a slipway down to the beach and the estuaries of the rivers Mite and Esk. Inaccessibility to everything but small craft, due to sandbars, meant that Ravenglass never developed as a port.

Nowadays, Ravenglass is synonymous with the Ravenglass and Eskdale Railway, affectionately known as 'Laal Ratty'. Though it is now one of the most popular visitor attractions in western Lakeland, the line has had a distinctly chequered career. The railway (with a 3-foot gauge track) was built in 1875, to carry iron ore (and a few passengers) from the Eskdale mines down to the coast and the main Furness line. When the mines became unprofitable, the railway closed.

Operating on a much narrower 15-inch gauge track, the line re-opened in 1913 to serve Eskdale's granite quarries and carry a few tourists. Trains plied the narrow-gauge track until they came to a halt once again, in 1953. Fortunately, a group of enthusiasts came to the rescue, helping to buy up the line in 1960, and running it as a tourist attraction. Today the miniature steam locos and carriages operate an extensive service over the seven highly scenic miles (11.2km) between Ravenglass and the terminus at Dalegarth. From any of the intervening five stations there is excellent walking country.

EFWARD

While many Roman sites in England were abandoned as soon as the invaders departed, and the dressed stone recycled for new building projects, the bath house buildings at Ravenglass had a longer life. During the 12th century they were almost certainly occupied by another invader, Norseman Efward, who counted Ravenglass among the many lands and possessions he appropriated. Efward is known to have built the first substantial bridge in the area, over the River Esk; he also founded a hospital for poor travellers.

WASDALE AND WAST WATER Map ref NY1606
The bleakly beautiful valley of Wasdale must be approached from the west, and for most visitors that necessitates a lengthy drive. The reward is that Wasdale will be spectacularly empty at times when the Lakeland 'honeypots' are straining under the weight of visitors.

If the view up to the head of the valley seems oddly familiar, that's because the National Park Authority created their logo from this view of Wast Water and the three peaks – Yewbarrow, Great Gable and Lingmell – whose symmetry frames the view. Scafell Pike, near the head of the valley is, at 3,210 feet (978m), the highest peak in England.

Although it is just 3 miles (4.8km) long, Wast Water is the deepest lake in England. The huge screes that dominate the southern shore continue their descent fully 250 feet (76m) into the cool clear waters. Those who tire of the speedboats rushing up and down busy Windermere – like so many amoebas under a microscope – will relish the tranquillity and awesome landscape of Wasdale.

The road hugs the water's edge until you reach Wasdale Head; communities don't come much smaller or more welcoming than this. The Wasdale Head Hotel is where walkers and climbers congregate to drink beer, take in some calories and swap tales of the mountains. Once you are ensconced in a comfortable chair it is easy to forget that you are miles from anywhere...

WASDALE HEAD CHURCH
Be sure to seek out Wasdale Head church. One of the smallest churches in the country, it is almost lost within a tiny copse of trees. Unadorned, like a barn, it may have been built as early as the 14th century. Legend suggests that the roof-beams were constructed out of timber taken from Viking ships. Before a restoration in 1892, there was an earth floor, few seats and no glass in the windows. An appropriate inscription in a tiny window reads: 'I will lift up mine eyes unto the hills'.

Great Gable is the conical peak at the head of Wast Water

A Ramble up the River Esk

This trail will take you into some of the wildest tracts of the Lake District. There are no difficult climbs, although there can be flooding, so it is wise to confirm conditions before starting. The walk will lead you to spectacular waterfalls and splendid views of Bow Fell and of Scafell Pike, the highest peak in England.

Time: 5 hours. Distance: 7½ miles (12.1km).
Location: 18 miles (29km) southeast of Whitehaven, 7 miles (11.3km) east of the A595 from Gosforth.
Start: From the car park adjacent to Dalegarth Station on the Ravenglass and Eskdale Railway. (OS grid ref: NY173007.)
OS Map: Outdoor Leisure 6 (The English Lakes – South Western area) 1:25,000.
See Key to Walks on page 121.

ROUTE DIRECTIONS

From Dalegarth Station on the **Ravenglass and Eskdale Railway** turn left up the valley road. Shortly, reach a crossroads with the village of Boot and the Burnmoor Inn arrowed left, and turn right into a walled lane leading to St Catherine's Church on the north bank of the Esk. Turn left at the church and walk along the river bank. At a bridge (do not cross) bear left through a wall on to a narrow walled track. This becomes a path traversing the hillside, just above the river, for half a mile (0.8km) before leading down and alongside the river to Doctor Bridge.

Go over the bridge and follow the farm road away from the River Esk towards Penny Hill Farm. Take the path around the farm and join a cart track. Go through some gates, take the left fork where the path divides. Keep to the track across fields, with Birker Fell towering ahead. To your left, further up the valley to the north you will see Bow Fell 2,959 feet (902m) and Scafell Pike 3,210 feet (978m). Ignore the footpath to Whahouse Bridge on your left, but bear left and cross a stream by a wooden footbridge and go through a gate in a wall. Walk through woodland and over stiles to cross a bracken-covered hillside until the path leads downhill and over a stream to the road at the bottom of the Hardknott Pass. High up on your right is the Roman fort of **Hardknott Castle**. Turn left over a cattle grid, go downhill, then right towards Brotherilkeld Farm

At the farmyard bear left and cross a small bridge into fields (do not cross the bridge over the River Esk). The path gradually climbs into the more untamed upper valley. To your left are Brock Crag and Heron Crag, while straight ahead stands Bow Fell. Continue to eventually reach the confluence of Lingcove Beck and the River Esk. Cross the beck by Lingcove Bridge and continue uphill to Esk Falls, where the water rushes down a boulder-filled course to tremendous effect. Cross the river by walking on the stones, but take care and do not try it in times of flooding (when it would be safest to retrace your steps to the footbridge at Brotherilkeld, crossing there to rejoin the route at Taw House Farm).

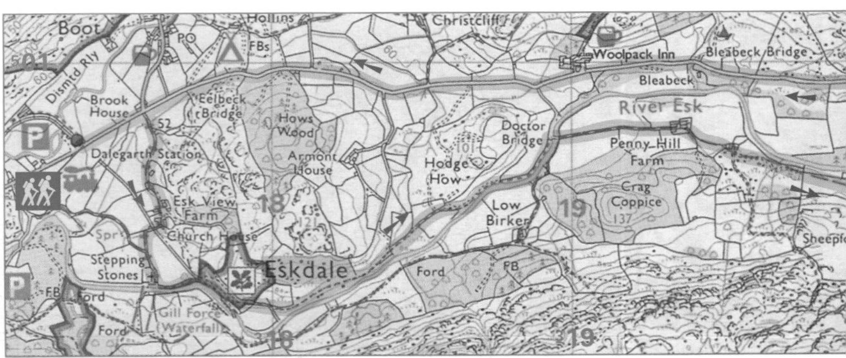

Having crossed to the other side, turn left and walk back down **Eskdale**. Traverse, without difficulty, some boggy land and reach a stone wall beneath Brock Crag. Continue right up the side of the hill, keeping the wall on your left and follow it above the river, past the waterfall and over Scale Bridge. Just before two stiles are two marked paths to Taw House. The upper one is better in wet conditions. From the farm follow the farm track down to Birdhow Cottage and the valley road. Turn right down the road for nearly 2 miles (3.2km) back to Dalegarth Station and the start of the walk.

POINTS OF INTEREST

Ravenglass and Eskdale Railway

This narrow-gauge (15-inch) miniature steam railway was opened in 1875 to carry iron ore from the mines at Boot to the Furness Railway on the coast. It is now a passenger line, where both steam and diesel locomotives are used during the summer to pull the open and saloon coaches through 7 miles (11.2km) of Eskdale countryside.

Hardknott Castle

Situated at the western end of Hardknott Pass, this Roman fort was built in the 2nd century AD and commands an isolated position overlooking Eskdale. The once walled and ramparted fort covered about three acres and the ruins include fragments of corner watchtowers and a bath house.

Eskdale

At its lower end this beautiful valley has a pastoral aspect, with bankside footpaths following the River Esk

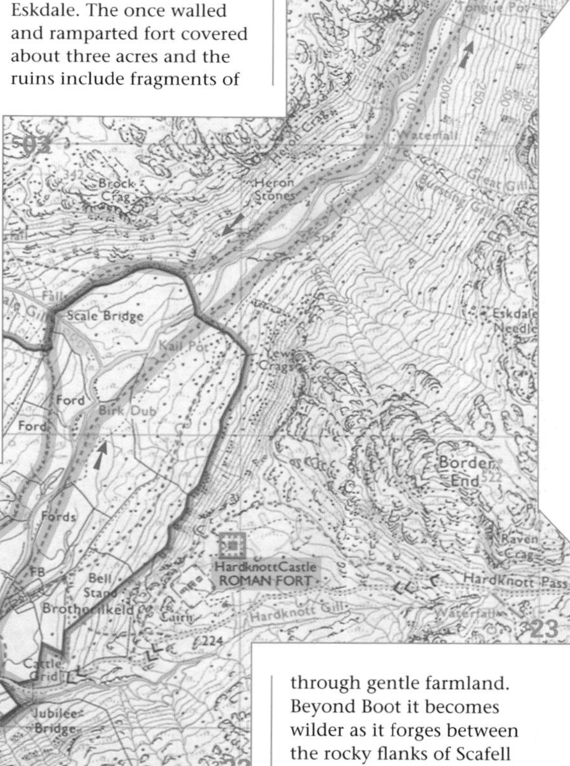

through gentle farmland. Beyond Boot it becomes wilder as it forges between the rocky flanks of Scafell Pike and Bow Fell.

The Roman fort at Hardknott successfully controlled the entire valley

Eskdale and Wasdale

Checklist

Leisure Information
Places of Interest
Shopping
The Performing Arts
Sports, Activities and the Outdoors
Annual Events and Customs

Leisure Information

TOURIST INFORMATION CENTRES

Barrow-in-Furness
Forum 28,
Duke Street.
Tel: 01229 894784.
Millom
Station Buildings.
Tel: 01229 774819.

A riveting display at Barrow's spectacular, modern Dock Museum, one of the town's most popular attractions

LAKE DISTRICT NATIONAL PARK INFORMATION POINTS

Boot
The Post Office.
Ravenglass
Ravenglass and Eskdale Railway Station.
Ulpha
Ulpha Post Office, Duddon Valley, near Broughton-in-Furness.
Wasdale Head
Barn Door Shop.

OTHER INFORMATION

Cumbria Wildlife Trust
Brockhole, Windermere.
Tel: 015394 48280.
English Heritage
Canada House, 3 Chepstow St, Manchester. Tel: 0161 242 1400
www.english-heritage.org.uk
Lake District National Park Authority Headquarters
Murley Moss, Oxenholme Road, Kendal. Tel: 01539 724555.
www.lake-district.gov.uk
National Trust in Cumbria
The Hollens, Grasmere, Ambleside, Cumbria. Tel: 015394 35599.
www.nationaltrust.org.uk
Public Transport
The Traveline service gives details of buses, boats, trains and ferries operating throughout Cumbria. Tel: 0870 608 2608.
Weather
Lake District Weather Service
Tel: 017687 75757.

ORDNANCE SURVEY MAPS

Landranger 1:50,000 Sheets 89, 95.
Outdoor Leisure: 1:25,000 Sheet 6.

Places of Interest

There will be an admission charge at the following places of interest unless otherwise stated.

The Ravenglass and Eskdale Railway passes by Muncaster Mill

Dock Museum
North Road, Barrow-in-Furness. Tel: 01229 894444. Open all year, certain days. Free.

Eskdale Mill
Boot. Tel: 019467 23335. Open Easter–Sep, most days.

Furness Abbey
Barrow-in-Furness. Tel: 01229 823420. Extensive remains of the Cistercian abbey built in 1147. Open all year, daily except Christmas and New Year's Day.

Hardknott Castle Roman Fort
Hardknott Pass. Remains of the Roman fort can be seen at the western end of Hardknott Pass. Open any reasonable time. Free.

Millom Folk Museum
Station Buildings, Millom. Tel: 01229 772555. Room sets include a miner's cottage and a blacksmith's forge. Open Easter to mid-Sep, most days.

Muncaster Castle, Gardens and Owl Centre
Muncaster. Tel: 01229 717614. Headquarters of the World Owl Trust. Castle open late Mar–Oct most days; garden and Owl Centre open all year, daily.

Muncaster Mill
Muncaster. Tel: 01229 717232. Flour and oatmeal are still ground on the premises. Open Apr–Oct, daily.

Ravenglass and Eskdale Railway
Ravenglass Tel: 01229 717171. Steam and diesel trains run along a 7-mile (11.2-km) track, through beautiful countryside, from Ravenglass to Dalegarth. They operate all year daily, except Christmas.

Ravenglass Roman Bath House
Ravenglass. Open all year. Free.

SPECIAL INTEREST FOR CHILDREN

The following places may be of interest to visitors with children. Unless otherwise stated, there will be an admission charge.

Millom Folk Museum
St George's Road, Millom. Tel: 01229 772555. Room sets include a miner's cottage and a blacksmith's forge. Open Easter to mid-Sep, most days.

Muncaster Castle, Gardens and Owl Centre
Muncaster. Tel: 01229 717614. Headquarters of the World Owl Trust. Castle open late Mar–Oct most days; garden and Owl Centre open all year, daily.

Ravenglass and Eskdale Railway
Ravenglass Tel: 01229 717171. Steam and diesel trains run along a 7-mile (11.2-km) track from Ravenglass to Dalegarth. The service operates all year daily, except Christmas.

South Lakes Wild Animal Park
Crossgates, Dalton-in-Furness. Tel: 01229 466086. Open all year daily, except Christmas Day.

Shopping

Barrow-in-Furness
Market, Wed, Fri and Sat.

Broughton-in-Furness
Market, Tue.

LOCAL SPECIALITIES

Crafts
The *Made in Cumbria* guide to workshops and galleries is available from Tourist Information Centres. Their web site lists over 400 members (craftspeople and artists) who produce everything from gifts to furniture and speciality foods, all made in Cumbria.
www.madeincumbria.co.uk

Cumberland Sausage
Award-winning sausage and

A road winds along the contours of the Duddon Valley by Ulpha

hams from Woodall's of Waberthwaite. Tel: 01229 717387.

Cumberland Rum Butter
Available from many local food shops.

Flour
Muncaster Mill, Muncaster. Tel: 01229 717232.
Flour and oatmeal are still ground on the premises. Open Apr–Oct daily.

Pottery
Dalton Pottery, 8 Nelson Street, Dalton-in-Furness. Tel: 01229 465313 (telephone before visit).
Gosforth Pottery, near Seascale Gosforth.
Tel: 019467 25296.

The Performing Arts

Forum 28 Theatre and Arts Centre
28 Duke Street, Barrow-in-Furness.
Tel: 01229 894489.

Sports, Activities and the Outdoors

SEA FISHING

There is good sea fishing from the shoreline around the Isle of Walney and Piel Island.
Sea fishing trips can be arranged by Mr S McCoy. Tel: 01229 826160.

BEACH

Silecroft and Haverigg
Extensive sandy beaches.

CYCLING

The Cumbria Cycle Way
Part of the 280-mile (450-km) route traverses the Furness peninsula. Details available from the local Tourist Information Centres.

GOLF COURSES

Askam-in-Furness
Dunnerholme, Duddon Road. Tel: 01229 462675.

Barrow-in-Furness
Barrow Golf Club, Rakesmoor Lane, Hawcoat. Tel: 01229 825444. Furness Golf Club, Central Drive, Isle of Walney. Tel: 01229 471232.

Silecroft
Silecroft Golf Club. Tel: 01229 774250.

GOLF DRIVING RANGE

Barrow-in-Furness
Stroke One Golf Driving, Hawthwaite Lane, near Roanhead. Tel: 01229 464164.

LONG-DISTANCE FOOTPATHS AND TRAILS

The Cistercian Way
A 33-mile (52.8-km) walk from Grange-over-Sands to Roa Island, near Barrow-in-Furness.

The Cumberland Way
An 82-mile (131.2-km) east to west crossing of the Lake District National Park from Ravenglass to Appleby.

The Cumbria Coastal Way
A 124-mile (198.4-km) walk from Barrow-in-Furness to Carlisle.

The Furness Boundary Walk
A 111-mile (177.6-km) circular walk from Barrow-in-Furness through Cumbria.

NATURE RESERVES

Haverigg Nature Reserve, near Millom.
North and South Walney Nature Reserves, Barrow-in-Furness.
Sandscales Haws, Barrow-in-Furness.

RUGBY

Barrow-in-Furness
Barrow Rugby League Football Club, Craven Park. Tel: 01229 820273.

Annual Events and Customs

Barrow-in-Furness
Barrow Horticultural Society Show, early September.

Eskdale
Eskdale Tup (ram) Show, late September.
Eskdale Show, late September.

Gosforth
Cumbria Riding Club Dressage Show, early April.
Gosforth Show, mid-August.
Cumbria Riding Club Hunter Trials, early October.

Millom
Millom and Broughton Agricultural Show, late August.

These checklists give details of just some of the facilities within the area covered by this guide. Further information can be obtained from Tourist Information Centres.

The Western Lakes

These western lakes and western shores of Cumbria tell a different story from other parts of Lakeland. Their features rival the most beautiful in the area – idyllic Buttermere and imposing Great Gable, to name but two – but this is also, in places, an industrial landscape. It is where men have carved coal, slate, and iron ore from beneath the green hills, to provide for their families and fuel the Industrial Revolution. Much of that fuel found its way through ports such as Maryport and Whitehaven. Today there are museums and heritage centres looking back on the past, and forming a fascinating contrast to the better-known face of the Lakes.

BUTTERMERE AND CRUMMOCK WATER

Map ref NY1716/NY1519

These two neighbouring lakes in the Buttermere valley, separated only by a half-mile (0.8km) strip of meadowland, were probably one lake originally. Buttermere is better known, and perhaps the more beautiful, although Crummock Water is twice its size. Its harsh-sounding name is Celtic, and means crooked,

You can walk right around the edge of Buttermere, on a 5-mile (8-km) footpath

CUMBERLAND RUM BUTTER

The name Buttermere comes from the area's rich dairy pastures. Cumberland Rum Butter is a concoction which combines the local produce with exotic imports from the West Indies, luxuries generated by the industrial trade of the 19th century. Rum, sugar, nutmeg and cinnamon were added to the butter and the result became a traditional gift to celebrate the birth of a baby, to wish a smooth but spirited life.

Looking northwest along the valley, Crummock Water comes into view behind Buttermere

THE MAID OF BUTTERMERE
Melvyn Bragg, author and broadcaster, wrote *The Maid of Buttermere,* which tells the story of Mary Robinson (Mary of Buttermere). Mary was the beautiful 15-year-old daughter of the innkeeper of the Fish Inn at Buttermere who was described in embarrassingly glowing terms, in 1795, by J Budworth in *A Fortnight's Ramble in the Lakes.* The poor girl became an early tourist attraction, and in 1802 married a supposed nobleman only to discover that he was a forger and a bigamist. He was hanged, Mary married a farmer and managed to lead a normal and happy life. She lived in Caldbeck, 16 miles (25.6km) northeast of Buttermere, and is buried in the local graveyard.

while the gentler Buttermere is named for the dairy pastures near by. Crummock Water can claim one of the most impressive waterfalls in the Lakes, Scale Force, on its western side, which plunges 172 feet (52m) on its way to the lake. The path to Scale Force, however, begins in tiny Buttermere village, and is a rough walk to the tree-lined gorge through which Scale Beck plummets.

A path leads all the way along Crummock Water's western shore, to join up with the B5289 which runs down the eastern shore. This road links Lorton Vale to the north of Buttermere, with the steep Honister Pass to the east, and continues on to Borrowdale. The dramatic pass is the site of a slate quarry and, although it is 1,167 feet (356m) high, it still manages to be overshadowed by the hills of well over 2,000 feet (610m) on either side. Some of the former slate workers' cottages can be seen in the village of Seatoller, at the far eastern end of the pass, where there is also a National Park Information Centre.

Buttermere is also surrounded by high hills, such as the 2,126-foot (648m) Fleetwith Pike which guards the Honister Pass and, close by, the 1,959-foot (597m) Hay Stacks. The easy two-hour walk around Buttermere is therefore an impressive one, with stunning views in all directions. To the northwest are the dramatic Derwent Fells, with Derwent Water beyond, while to the west above Burtness Wood stand a range of crags and fells. Most of the land around both Buttermere and Crummock Water is, these days, owned by the National Trust, and both lakes are within the National Park boundaries, so their unspoilt beauty seems secure for future generations.

COCKERMOUTH Map ref NY1230

For a small country market town, Cockermouth has plenty of history behind it. The most significant event as far as most of today's visitors are concerned is that William Wordsworth was born here in 1770. If you first visit modest Dove Cottage in Grasmere, where the poet later lived, the grandeur of his birthplace, a Georgian town house dating from 1745, comes as a surprise. Wordsworth House has been faithfully restored by the National Trust and has seven rooms – including a spotless kitchen and an elegant drawing room with an original fireplace – furnished in mid-18th century style, with some of Wordsworth's own personal effects.

Many more famous names are associated with Cockermouth, however, including the mutineer on *The Bounty*, Fletcher Christian, also born near by. Mary, Queen of Scots and Robert the Bruce both passed through, the former simply to spend the night after the Battle of Langside in 1568, the latter with more of a purpose. In 1315 Bruce destroyed part of the 12th-century castle, built by the English in the hope of keeping the marauding Scots out of this important market town, which had gained its charter in 1221. Earlier, the Romans had used Cockermouth as a strategic stronghold (it was at the confluence of the Rivers Cocker and Derwent) to control the Iron-Age Brigante tribes who inhabited the north at the time.

The town now houses a printing museum, a toy and model museum, the William Creighton Minerals and Fossil Museum, an art gallery at Castlegate House and Jennings' Brewery, which dates from 1828 and offers hour-long guided tours.

NAMING PLACES

It ought to be obvious that Cockermouth's name is due to its location at the mouth of the River Cocker, but there is slightly more to it than that. The 'mot' ending describes a meeting of waters, so it may be where a river meets the sea or, as in this case, where two rivers meet. The author of an interesting booklet 'Walks Round the Town', local historian J B Bradbury, points out that the name was Cocremuth in 1222 and recorded as Cockermua in 1215. The 'Cocker' part was 'Koker' in 1170, and means crooked, the word having evolved slightly differently at Crummock Water, the Crooked Lake.

LAKELAND SHEEP AND WOOL CENTRE

On the A66, close to Cockermouth, visitors can meet local and other breeds of sheep which 'take the stage' four times daily from Easter to mid-November. Shearing and dog work is demonstrated and there is a Cumwest Visitor Centre.

William Wordsworth was born in this Georgian house in Cockermouth in 1770

From the Mouth of the Crooked River

This tour of 58 miles (93km) starts at Cockermouth, which is famous for being the birthplace of Wordsworth. It continues to the coast at Maryport, before heading north, hugging the coastline and passing through small fishing villages and a designated Area of Outstanding Natural Beauty. The route then turns inland, taking in small villages and pretty market towns, crossing the boundary of the National Park and finally returning to Cockermouth.

ROUTE DIRECTIONS

See Key to car Tours on page 120.

In Cockermouth take the time to walk around and breathe in some of the character of the area — visit **Wordsworth House** (the poet's birthplace) which is in Main Street. The 13th-century Norman castle here is now partially ruined but a section of it is still inhabited by the Egremont family; however, the castle is rarely open to the public.

Take the A594 out of Cockermouth and drive for 7 miles (11.2km) to Maryport. A port in Roman times, it was developed in the 18th century by Humphrey Senhouse. Visit the harbour, marina, **Maritime Museum** and **Aquarium**, then go up the hill to the Roman Museum and look out over the town.

Leave Maryport on the A596 Carlisle road, then turn left on the B5300 and continue for 2 miles (3.2km) to a car park on the right for **Saltpans**, the site of a 17th-century saltworks and a Roman milecastle. Continue to Allonby, which retains much of its appeal from when it developed as a Georgian and Victorian bathing resort. Across the Solway you can see Scotland and the Galloway hills.

From Allonby continue

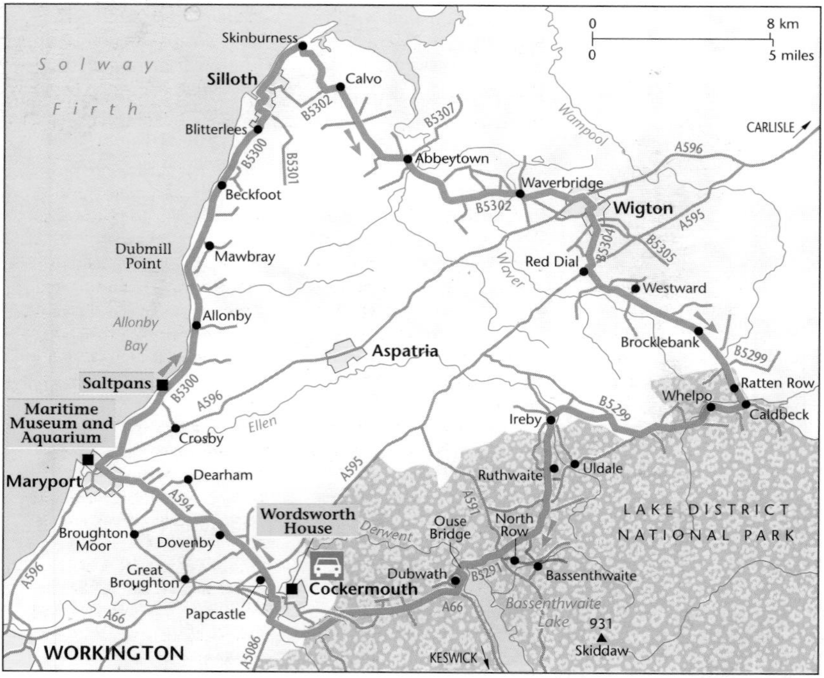

Huntsman John Peel, made famous by the song 'De ye Ken John Peel', died in 1854 and was buried in Caldbeck churchyard

north for 6 miles (9.6km) on the B5300 to Silloth. Until 1857 Silloth was a small fishing village, then it expanded as a port when linked by rail with Carlisle; the town still preserves its Victorian spa atmosphere. Continue straight on past the green and drive for about 1½ miles (2.4km) to Skinburness. This area of the Solway Firth is designated an Area of Outstanding Natural Beauty.

Continue on a narrow road from Skinburness for a further 2 miles (3.2km). Turn left on to the B5302 and drive through Calvo to Abbeytown. Once an important town with an abbey which is one of the few that survived Henry VIII's Dissolution of the Monasteries, but in the guise of a parish church. In the graveyard is the tombstone of the father of Robert the Bruce, buried here in 1294, 25 years before his son sacked the abbey.

Leave Abbeytown on the B5302, then just beyond Waverbridge turn left on to an unclassified road, signed Aikhead and Station Hill. On reaching the A596, turn left and then right into Wigton and soon right again into the town centre, where a feature of this pleasant market town is the gilded granite fountain, which is dedicated to the memory of George Moore, who made his fortune in London.

Leave Wigton by turning left in the town centre signed B5305 and then soon B5304. In about a mile (1.6km) cross the A595 and continue for about 7 miles (11.2km) on an unclassified road, to arrive in Caldbeck on the B5299. To visit Caldbeck park close to the church or adjacent Priest's Mill where there is a tea room. This is an attractive village with a green, duck pond and the ancient Church of St Kentigern. The gravestone of the famous huntsman, John Peel, is near the church on the left.

Leave Caldbeck in the direction by which you entered the town, but this time bear left on B5299 (to the left of the Oddfellow's Arms). After about 3 miles (5km), over moorland, at a fork keep to the B5299 and continue for another mile to a sign for Ireby. Turn left and descend into the village, turn left again and follow the signs for Bassenthwaite. Here, for the first time, you enter the Lake District National Park.

Continue to reach a junction where a road from Uldale comes in on the left. Continue down to meet the A591. Turn right, then left in front of the Castle Inn Hotel on to the B591.

Keep ahead on the B5291 and once over Ouse Bridge turn left to where there is parking. This is good place to stop and take a break and a stroll in beautiful scenery.

Continue on the B5291 for about half a mile (0.8 km) to meet the A66, turn right and drive back on it to Cockermouth.

WHAT CRABS?

The crabs at the Egremont Crab Fair are crab apples not crustaceans. The fair dates from 1267, and on the third Saturday in September the Apple Cart parade passes through the town, and apples are thrown to people lining the route. Today they are eating apples, not crab apples. There are athletics competitions, animal shows, hound trails and a greasy pole competition. In the evening is the event which everyone knows about – the World Gurning Championship. It is more accurately called the Gurning through a Braffin competition, and whoever can make the ugliest grin (gurn) while peering through a horse collar (a braffin), is declared world champion, if only because no one else in the world does it.

The landscape of Ennerdale is best explored on foot

EGREMONT Map ref NY0110

With the River Ehen winding through it, and a wide main street lined with trees (and with a variety of stalls on its Friday market day), Egremont is a pretty town renowned as the home of ugly faces. For it is here that the World Gurning Championships are held each September. The country fair in which they take place is almost as old as Egremont Castle, whose ruins stand in a park on a hilltop overlooking that wide main street. This Norman building of red sandstone dates from the 12th century, though it was largely destroyed in the 16th century; its best surviving feature is the original gatehouse.

Dating from the 16th century is the Lowes Court Gallery on Main Street, restored for the promotion of local arts and crafts. Jewellery made from haematite, the local red iron ore, can be bought at the nearby Florence Mine Heritage Centre. This is the last deep working iron-ore mine in Europe, where you will find out why the miners are known as the Red Men of Cumbria. Mining conditions at the turn of the century have been recreated in the Heritage Centre, and a small museum tells the history of the mine.

ENNERDALE Map ref NY1015

Walkers may appreciate Ennerdale Water more than many other lakes, as access by car is limited and the bulk of its shores can only be explored on foot. Lying in the secluded valley of Ennerdale, its shores are well worth exploring – from the car park at Bowness Knott, a path leads east along the forested northern side of the lake. The land around Ennerdale Water was bought by the Forestry Commission in 1926, and planting began the

following year. Behind the rows of spruce and larch, the land rises steeply, to over 2,600 feet (793m) in places. Looking south the hills are higher still, with Pillar at 2,926 feet (892m), in front of which Pillar Rock is still used by climbers since its first ascent in 1826.

Ennerdale Water is, in fact, a reservoir serving west Cumbria, and it is possible to walk all the way round, although the going is tough in places and the whole route is 8 miles (12.8km) long.

GREAT GABLE Map ref NY2110

There are higher mountains than Great Gable's 2,949 feet (899m), but visually it holds its own. If approaching from the southwest from Wast Water and through Wasdale Head, its bulk resembles the great gable end of a house. This imposing approach, which is tough but readily accessible to fit walkers, is one route up to the top. Another is from the northeast, from Seathwaite Farm (see Walk on page 64), climbing up past the waters of the wonderfully named Sourmilk Gill and passing Great Gable's little brother, Green Gable.

At the top is a plaque which proudly records the occasion when the surrounding area was given to the National Trust by members of the Fell and Rock Climbing Club, in memory of their colleagues lost in World War I. A service is held here each year on Remembrance Sunday. It was in these hills which you can see around you that the modern sport of climbing first started to develop, late in the 19th century. The names alone are inspiring: Needle Ridge, Eagle's Nest Ridge, Windy Gap. The view still inspires, south to Scafell Pike 3,210 feet (978m) and straight down Wasdale towards the Irish Sea.

A GREAT CLIMBER

On the southern slopes of Great Gable's peak is the slim pinnacle of rock known as Napes Needle. The first to climb this, in 1886, was 24-year-old Walter Parry Haskett-Smith, who became something of a legend among climbers. An indication to non-climbers of why he is so highly regarded is the fact that he climbed the same rock again in 1936, by which time he was 74 years of age.

Great Gable, seen here behind the pointed peak of Yewbarrow, from Wast Water, is a distinctive landmark in the region

Great Gable

Great Gable is probably one of the best known peaks in the Lake District and it is encompassed by countryside that is as dramatic and varied as anywhere in Britain. This is a serious and energetic walk going up to 2,949 feet (899m) with the need to ensure that you have proper clothing and footwear (and a compass) suitable for all weather conditions.

Time: 4–5 hours. Distance: 5 miles (8km).
Location: Seathwaite. A farmstead located at the end of an unclassified lane towards the top of Borrowdale, 1½ miles (2.4km) off the B5289 south of Keswick at Seatoller.
Start: Seathwaite Farm. Park on the roadside leading down to the farm. (OS grid ref: NY235122.)
OS Map: Outdoor Leisure 4 (The English Lakes – North Western area) 1:25,000.
See Key to Walks on page 121.

ROUTE DIRECTIONS

From the farmyard at **Seathwaite Farm** turn right under the archway and follow the lane to the footbridge over a stream. Ahead, **Sourmilk Gill** plunges down over 1,000 feet (305m) of rock. Beyond the footbridge, bear left to reach a stile over a wall. Climb the stile and ascend the path that follows the south bank of Sourmilk Gill. Eventually follow the path left through a gate in a wall, with views away to your left of Base Brown Fell. Keep to the defined path as it steadily ascends to the left around the foot of Base Brown, leading you into the upland valley of Gillercomb (Snares Valley). Towering over the valley, to your right, is the impressive Raven Crag.

Soon emerge out of Gillercomb and reach the dip that separates Base Brown from Green Gable. Your path continues to climb, bearing right over rough ground to a wide grassy ridge to the left of a conspicuous outcrop of rock. Merge with a path that comes from the far side of the outcrop, and follow this worn trail left, uphill to the summit of Green Gable. From here you will be confronted by Gable Crag across Windy Gap with Kirk Fell to its right. In the gap between Great Gable and Kirk Fell you can see Seatallen in the distance.

Bear left off the summit and follow the abrupt, stony path down into Windy Gap. On the far bank, climb to the left along a path to reach the base of steeper ground. Here, a rocky trail will lead you up to the boulders that make up Great Gable. From the summit of **Great Gable**, weather permitting, you can see the Isle of Man, from where many of the Vikings came to settle in Cumbria. For better views make your way, with care, to Westmorland Cairn on top of Westmorland Crag, located just southwest from the summit. To descend from Great Gable, walk southeastwards, or initially to the left as you look at the

The lop-sided arch of Stockley Bridge blends into its rocky surroundings

memorial plate to those of the Fell and Rock Club who died in World War I.

Proceed down the path to reach Styhead Pass, near the Mountain Rescue box. Turn left and follow the wide path past Styhead Tarn and continue along this path on the left bank of Styhead Gill until you reach the footbridge over the gill. Cross the bridge and descend on a worn path to eventually cross **Stockley Bridge**. From the bridge, bear left and continue downhill into the valley and return to Seathwaite Farm.

POINTS OF INTEREST

Seathwaite Farm
Nestling at the end of the road in the heart of Borrowdale, considered by many to be the most beautiful valley in the Lake District, this farmstead and its immediate area has the unenviable reputation of being the wettest inhabited spot in England, with an average of 131 inches (333cm) of rain a year.

Sourmilk Gill
The waterfall Sourmilk Gill probably takes its name from the white froth which is created by the steep drop – over 1,000 feet (303m) – to the floor of the valley.

Great Gable
The Norse name for this fell was Mykelgavel, which means the same thing as great gable, and probably refers to the shape of the fell, which looks like the gable of a house.

Stockley Bridge
The bridge was destroyed by floods in August 1966 and has since been painstakingly rebuilt. Stockley means a wooded clearing and reminds us that this area was at one time covered in trees.

Conservation
This walk covers miles of stone-pitched paths which were created by the National Trust to combat severe erosion.

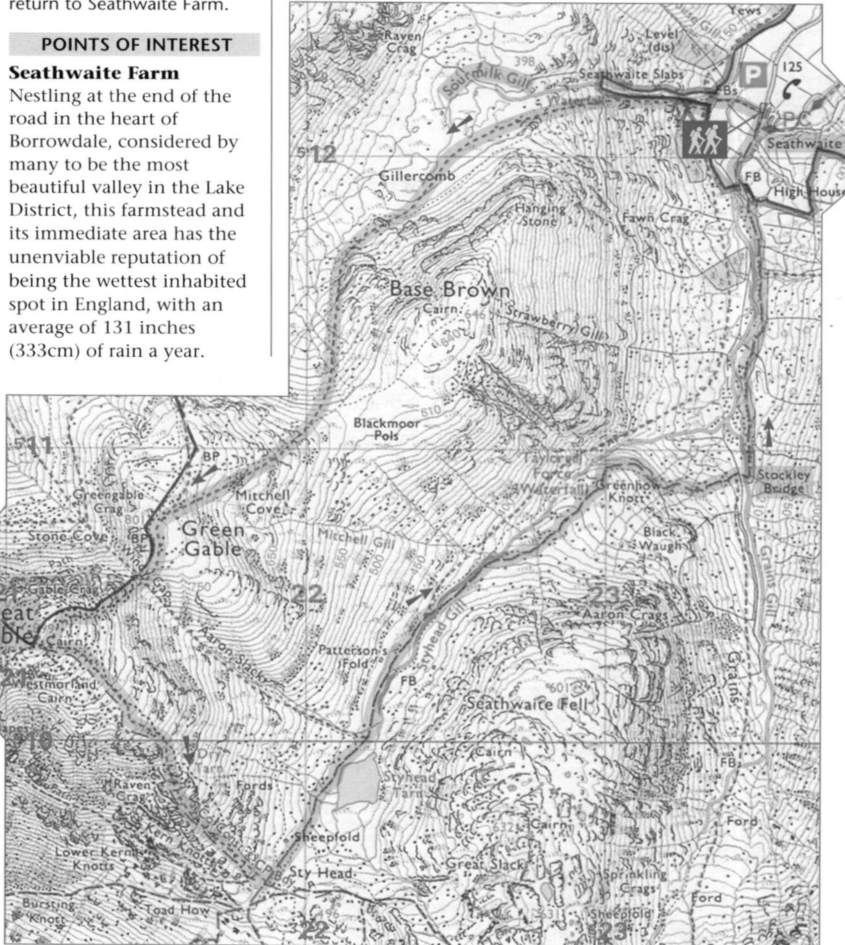

A colourful trio of cottages at Lorton

QUAKER FOX

George Fox preached in Lorton and pretty well anywhere else where he would be heard. He was born in Leicestershire in 1624 and wandered the country spreading his beliefs, having rebelled against the formal nature of the established Church and the fact that it was controlled by the State. Instead he founded his Society of Friends, or the Quakers, who keep Fox's creed today with their informal approach to religion. Fox also took his own brand of faith to Europe, America and the West Indies. He died in 1691.

LORTON Map ref NY1625

Lorton Vale is the valley which sweeps south from Cockermouth and passes the village of Loweswater, Crummock Water and finally Buttermere before ending in the lofty Honister Pass. Five miles (8km) south-east of Cockermouth is the village of Lorton, which is divided in two. High Lorton clings to the side of Kirk Fell at the start of the Whinlatter Pass, and is famous for its yew tree. This magnificent tree which stands behind the village hall (known as Yew Tree Hall, of course) was described by Wordsworth in his poem, 'Yew Trees'. It is further celebrated because it was beneath its boughs that the founder of the Quaker movement, George Fox, preached to a large crowd under the watchful eyes of Cromwell's soldiers.

Low Lorton straggles down the hill to the River Cocker, on whose banks stands Lorton Hall. This is privately owned but visits are possible if arrangements are made in advance. It has a 15th-century pele tower and its own chapel, with priest holes inside the Hall and much handsome oak panelling and furniture.

LOWESWATER Map ref NY1221

All Lake District lakes seem to have at least one feature that is special to them – the deepest, the longest, the highest – and Loweswater's claim is that it is the only lake whose waters flow inland, draining into Crummock Water. It is one of the smaller lakes but is no less delightful for that, being often less crowded than those lakes of easier access. To reach it involves a short drive on the B5289 down Lorton Vale from Cockermouth, but many motorists continue down the main road which leads them to Crummock Water and Buttermere. Instead, take a turning through Brackenthwaite which leads along the north shore of the lake with parking at either end. Loweswater is surrounded by woodland and meadows, where sheep graze on the lush grass. The woods are owned by the National Trust and have many leafy paths through them.

MARYPORT Map ref NY0336

A comparatively new Cumbrian town, founded only in 1749, Maryport was intended to serve as a port for the coal trade and was named after Mary, the wife of the Lord of the Manor, Humphrey Senhouse II. The port grew, and for a while was the biggest port in Cumberland, with trade from the iron-ore mines and also a healthy ship-building industry. The story of its rise and subsequent decline is told in the Maryport Maritime Museum, which also has exhibits ranging from a whale's tooth to telescopes. The museum is in Senhouse Street which leads to Elizabeth Dock. Instead of working ships, here you will now find Maryport Steamships. The *Flying Buzzard*, a 1951 tugboat from the Clyde Shipping Company, has been refitted to show visitors what life aboard a tug was like, until this one sank. The VIC *96* display shows a VIC (Victualler Inshore Craft) steamship from World War II, with lots of fun aboard – have a go at climbing into a hammock, raising a sail or building up your strength with a block and tackle.

The Senhouse Roman Museum has collections dating from 1570, when John Senhouse rescued some pieces from Maryport's Roman fort. It was added to by the family over the centuries, with some fine examples of Roman altars, and these are now on show in the Battery, an old naval building on the edge of the town.

THE 'UNSINKABLE' TITANIC

Thomas Henry Ismay, one of Maryport's successful sons, founded the great White Star Line. Unfortunately they will go down (as indeed did their ship) as the company which built the *Titanic*. On its maiden voyage from Liverpool to New York in April 1912, the luxury liner struck an iceberg just before midnight on 14th April, and about two-thirds of the people on board were killed, which resulted in 1,513 deaths. Before sailing, the ship had been described as 'unsinkable'. Maryport's Maritime Museum tells the story.

Visitors are invited to step aboard the old steam tug* Flying Buzzard *at Maryport Maritime Museum

Wild flowers cling to the precipitous red sandstone cliffs at St Bees Head

ST BEES Map ref NX9711

St Bees is the start of Wainwright's famous 190-mile (304km) Coast-to-Coast walk to Robin Hood's Bay in North Yorkshire, not to mention a coast-to-coast cycle route, and it lies on the Cumbria Cycle Way, too. Popular with walkers, therefore, it is a pleasant village in which to linger before heading off to the east. Before you go inland, take time to explore the impressive sandstone cliffs of St Bees Head, which rise to 462 feet (141m) and which lead to the lighthouse looking over Saltom Bay towards Whitehaven. This part of the coast is Cumbria's only Heritage Coast, with land on the cliffs forming the St Bees Head Nature Reserve. Watch out for puffins, razorbills and kittiwakes, as well as the black guillemot which breeds nowhere else in England.

In the village itself is the Church of Saint Mary and Saint Bega which dates back to about AD 650, when it was part of a priory, though its most striking feature is the impressive Norman door, from 1160, its arches fanning out like a peacock's tail. St Bees also has its own beach, with several other beaches south along the coast. Six miles (9.6km) southeast of St Bees is the Sellafield Nuclear Power Station and its Visitor Centre, where visitors are treated to a thoroughly professional series of displays explaining the Sellafield story and the virtues of nuclear power. Children will enjoy trying to create electricity by pedal power, and they can even bring home sticks of Sellafield rock for their friends.

KNIGHT COMES TO LIGHT

The name of St Bees comes from St Bega, an Irish saint who founded the priory in the 7th century. When excavations were made near here in the 1980s, a lead coffin was found which contained the very well-preserved mummified remains of a body thought to be that of a 13th-century knight. Such was the state of preservation that the blood in the body's veins was still semi-liquid. After examination at West Cumberland Hospital, the body was reburied.

WHITEHAVEN Map ref NX9718

In the middle of the 18th century Whitehaven was the third largest port in Britain, after London and Bristol, thanks to the local industries. The coal mines of Workington and Maryport, just to the north, were also thriving showing the importance of that industry to Cumbria's west coast towns. Today Whitehaven has a small fishing fleet, and its harbour has been declared a conservation area, with several monuments to its past mining history, which finally died out in 1986. Your first stop in Whitehaven should be The Beacon, on West Strand, which offers visitors an insight into the history of the town and harbour using audio-visual presentations and exciting displays. On the top floor is the Weather Gallery full of high-tech equipment which monitors and records the weather.

The town also boasts many handsome Georgian buildings and has two churches that are worth seeking out. St Begh's dates from around 1868 and is visually striking as it was built from white stone with a red stone dressing. St James' is slightly older, from 1753, with Italian ceiling designs and a very moving Memorial Chapel. It was dedicated first to those who lost their lives in the two world wars, and later also to local people – men, women and children – who were killed in mining accidents. A miner's lamp serves as the Sanctuary lamp.

Book lovers should note that Whitehaven harbours the largest antiquarian bookshop in Cumbria, and one of the largest in the north of England. Michael Moon's Bookshop and Gallery in Roper Street claims to have 100,000 books on its mile (1.6km) of shelving, with room for at least 100 book browsers at the same time.

CYCLING ALL THE WAY

Mountainous Cumbria might not seem the best place for cyclists, but there are some fairly flat parts, especially near the coast. That is the route taken by the Cumbria Cycle Way, while the West Cumbria Cycle Network runs 10 miles (16km) from Whitehaven close to the villages of Arlecdon and Rowrah, where it joins the minor roads for a final short stretch to Ennerdale. The off-road section takes the route of the former Whitehaven–Rowrah railway

THE RUM STORY

Whitehaven was once a centre of the rum trade. The story of how it is made, and of its links with slavery and smuggling, is told in the original 1785 shop and bonded warehouses in Lowther Street.

The Beacon, at Whitehaven, houses a sophisticated weather station

A Taste of the Past at Cleator Moor

An easy walk through what was for years a scene of industrial dereliction. Imaginative restoration and conservation have acheived a remarkable transformation. But for the industrial archaeologist evidence becomes harder to find, and in some cases is symbolic rather than real.

Time: 1½ hours. Distance: 2 miles (3.2km).
Location: Cleator Moor. Situated on the B5295, 6 miles (9.6km) southeast of Whitehaven.
Start: Cleator Moor Square in town centre. Adequate parking in the square. (OS grid ref: NY019149.)
OS Map: Explorer 303 (Whitehaven & Workington) 1:25,000.
See Key to Walks on page 121.

ROUTE DIRECTIONS

From **Cleator Moor** Square, walk along the High Street in the direction of Whitehaven, keeping to the left-hand side of the road. Go down the hill passing a small garden and park – once the site of Montreal School and Montreal Street, which were demolished due to mine subsidence during World War II. Continue to an opening on your left with metal barriers and a sculpture and pass through it to join the old railway line, which you follow to the left. It is part of the **West Cumbria Cyclepath Link**, a 10-mile (16km) route from Whitehaven to Ennerdale.

Before going left, note that about here was the Crowgarth Mine with at least seven shafts. By the bridge to your right (its metal sculpture is a reminder of past industry) were two other mines – Montreal No 1 and No 6. Time and vegetation make this anything but obvious.

Continuing left, away from the bridge, pass a number of metal and stone creations redolent of the area's past. The path is popular with local strollers and older ones may be pleased to share with you the story of the area's former network of mines, works and railways.

After the way curves right, views open up to the Ennerdale fells. Keep on until, by a stone bench with an inscribed stone behind, turn right on to yet another old railway line. Following this you pass the site of Montreal No 12 mine and ahead, beyond a fenced area, are the remains of No 4 mine which

The area around Cleator Moor is littered with derelict monuments to 19th-century industry

The Church of St John at Cleator Moor is unforgiving in style, but built of the local warm red sandstone

produced both iron ore and coal. Keep straight on and pass through another metal gate into Leconfield Street. Turn right and follow the road back to the town centre.

POINTS OF INTEREST

Cleator Moor

Cleator is an odd-sounding name and comes from the Norse words for cliff and hill pasture. The town of Cleator Moor developed rapidly in the 19th century, as the Industrial Revolution demanded more and more coal and high grade iron ore. But before World War I supplies had already begun to decline. The raw materials mined at Cleator Moor were mainly used in local furnaces. Around the town and cycleway look out for the imaginative metal sculptures – many reflect the area's industrial history.

The West Cumbria Cyclepath Network

Includes a 10-mile (16km) route which runs from the port of Whitehaven to near the villages of Arlecdon and Rowrah, where it joins a minor road to Ennerdale. The off-road section of the route is on the former Whitehaven–Rowrah railway which was part of a network built in the late 1850s to link the mines and the quarries with the iron works at Whitehaven and Workington.

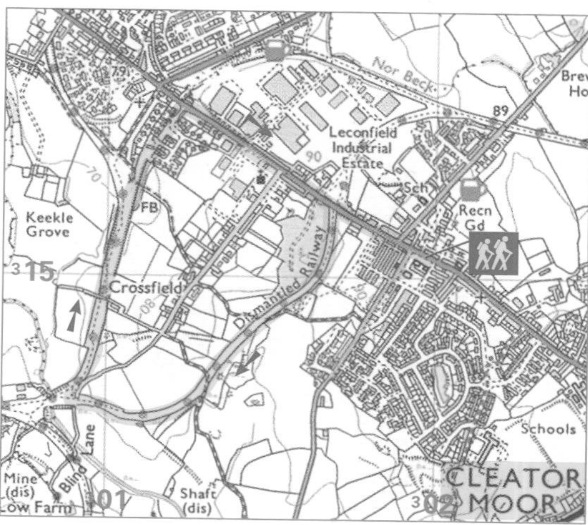

The Western Lakes

Checklist

Leisure Information
Places of Interest
Shopping
The Performing Arts
Sports, Activities and the Outdoors
Annual Events and Customs

Leisure Information

TOURIST INFORMATION CENTRES

Cockermouth
The Town Hall. Tel: 01900 822634.
Egremont
Lowes Court Gallery, 12 Main Street. Tel: 01946 820693.
Maryport
Maryport Maritime Museum, 1 Senhouse Street. Tel: 01900 813738.
Whitehaven
Market Hall, Market Place.
Tel: 01946 852939.
Workington
Carnegie Theatre Foyer, Finkle Street.
Tel: 01900 606699.

LAKE DISTRICT NATIONAL PARK INFORMATION POINTS

Ennerdale
Ennerdale Bridge Post Office.
Gosforth
Gosforth Pottery.
High Lorton
The Post Office.
St Bees
The Post Office, 122 Main Street.

OTHER INFORMATION

Cumbria Wildlife Trust
Brockhole, Windermere.
Tel: 015394 48280.
English Heritage
Canada House, 3 Chepstow Street, Manchester.
Tel: 0161 242 1400.
www.english-heritage.org.uk
Groundwork West Cumbria
48 High Street, Cleator Moor.
Tel: 01946 813677.
Information on innovative conservation initiatives.
Lake District National Park Authority Headquarters
Murley Moss, Oxenholme Road, Kendal. Tel: 01539 724555.
www.lake-district.gov.uk
National Trust in Cumbria
The Hollens, Grasmere, Ambleside, Cumbria.
Tel: 015394 35599.
www.nationaltrust.org.uk
Public Transport
The Traveline service gives details of buses, boats, trains and ferries operating throughout Cumbria.
Tel: 0870 608 2608.
Weather
Lake District Weather Service.
Tel: 017687 75757.

ORDNANCE SURVEY MAPS

Landranger 1:50,000
Sheet 89.
Outdoor Leisure 1:25,000
Sheet 4.

Places of Interest

There will be an admission charge at the following places of interest unless otherwise stated.

The Beacon
West Strand, Whitehaven. Tel: 01946 592302. Exciting displays, hands-on exhibits and audio-visual presentations bring to life the history of the town and harbour. Open all year, most days.
Castlegate House Gallery
Cockermouth. Tel: 01900 822149. Open Mar–Dec, most days. Free.
Florence Mine Heritage Centre
Egremont. Tel: 01946 820683. Open Apr–Oct, daily.
Flying Buzzard* and VIC *96
Elizabeth Dock, South Quay, Maryport Harbour, Maryport. Tel: 01900 815954 for details of opening times.
Helena Thompson Museum
Park End Road, Workington. Tel: 01900 326255. Small museum displaying costumes, glass and ceramics and items of local historical interest. Open all year, most days. Free.
Jennings Brewery
Castle Brewery, Cockermouth. Tel: 01900 821011. Tours all

year, most days. No children under the age of 12.

Lakeland Sheep and Wool Centre & Cumwest Visitor Centre
Egremont Road, Cockermouth. Tel: 01900 822673. Open all year, daily.

Lowes Court Gallery
12 Main Street, Egremont. Tel: 01946 820693. Open all year, most days. Free.

Maryport Aquaria
South Quay, Maryport. Tel: 01900 817760. Open all year, daily.

Maryport Maritime Museum
1 Senhouse Street, Maryport. Tel: 01900 813738. Models and paintings illustrating Maryport's maritime traditions. Open daily in summer, most days in winter.

The Printing House
102 Main Street, Cockermouth. Tel: 01900 824984. Open all year, most days.

The Rum Story
Lowther Street, Whitehaven. Tel: 01946 592933. Open all year, daily, except 25 Dec and 1 Jan.

The Sellafield Visitor Centre
Signposted off A595. Tel: 019467 27027. Open all year, daily except Christmas Day.

Senhouse Roman Museum
The Battery, Sea Brows, Maryport. Tel: 01900 816168. Open all year, certain days; Jul–Sep daily.

The William Creighton Mineral and Fossil Museum
Crown Street, Cockermouth. Tel: 01900 828301 Open early Apr–late Dec most days.

Wordsworth House
Main Street, Cockermouth. Tel: 01900 824805. Open Apr–Oct most days.

Workington Hall
Workington. Tel: 01900 326408. Open Easter–Oct most days.

SPECIAL INTEREST FOR CHILDREN

The following places may be of interest to visitors with children. Unless otherwise stated, there will be an admission charge.

The Beacon
West Strand, Whitehaven. Tel: 01946 592302. Open all year, most days.

The Cumberland Toy and Model Museum
Banks Court, Market Place, Cockermouth. Tel: 01900 827606. Open Feb–Nov daily.

Flying Buzzard* and *VIC 96
Elizabeth Dock, South Quay, Maryport Harbour, Maryport. Tel: 01900 815954. Telephone for details of opening times.

Lakeland Sheep and Wool Centre
See previous column.

Maryport Aquarium
See previous column.

Sellafield Visitor Centre
See previous column.

St Nicholas Church Tower
Whitehaven. Climb the spiral staircase and wind the 18th-century clock. Open most days.

Shopping

Egremont
Open-air market, Fri.

Maryport
Open-air market, Fri.

Whitehaven
Open-air market, Thu and Sat. Michael Moon Antiquarian, Second-hand books. 41–2 Roper Street. Tel: 01946 62936.

Workington
Open-air market, Wed and Sat.

LOCAL SPECIALITIES

Beer
Jennings beers, available in many local pubs.

Cumberland Rum Butter
Available in local shops.

The Performing Arts

Carnegie Theatre and Arts Centre
Finkle Street, Workington. Tel: 01900 602122.

Civic Hall
Whitehaven. Tel: 01946 852821.

Rosehill Theatre
Moresby, Whitehaven. Tel: 01946 692422.

Sports, Activities and the Outdoors

ANGLING

For information about fishing the lakes and rivers contact local tourist information centres or the NationalTrust. Tel: 015394 35599.

Coarse
Loweswater Water End Farm. Tel: 01946 861465.

BEACHES

Allonby
Sand and shingle.

Beckfoot
Sand and shingle.

St Bees
Sand and shingle. Fleswick Bay, shingle cove, sand at low tide.

Silloth
Sand and shingle. Bathing not safe when tide is ebbing.

BOAT HIRE

Loweswater
Water End Farm. Tel: 01946 861465.

CYCLING

The Coast-to-Coast Cycle Route
A 140-mile (224-km) route linking Whitehaven and

A sturdy fishing boat moored in the harbour at Whitehaven

A pleasing combination of pink and grey cobbles completes Maryport's Fleming Square

Workington in the west to Sunderland (Tyne and Wear) in the east.

The Cumbria Cycle Way
A 280-mile (450-km) almost circular route around the border of Cumbria. Information available from local Tourist Information Centres.

The Reivers Cycle Route
A 190-mile (306-km) quiet country route from Tynemouth to Whitehaven. Maps are available from Tourist Information Centres.

West Cumbria Cycle Network
A network of cycle routes using disused railways and minor roads. Maps from local Tourist Information Centres.

CYCLE HIRE

Wigton
Wigton Cycle & Sports, 23 West Street. Tel: 016973 42824.
See also Keswick page 85.

GO-KARTING

Maryport
West Coast Indoor Karting, Solway Trading Estate. Maryport.
Tel: 01900 816472.

GOLF COURSES

Cockermouth
Cockermouth Golf Club, Embleton. Tel: 017687 76223.

Maryport
Maryport Golf Club, Bank End. Tel: 01900 812605.

St Bees
St Bees Golf Club. Tel: 01946 824300. (9-hole).

Seascale
Seascale Golf Club, The Banks. Tel: 019647 28202.

Workington
Workington Golf Club, Branthwaite Road. Tel: 01900 603460.

HORSE-RIDING

Gilcrux
Allonby Riding School.
Tel: 016973 22889.

Ennerdale
Bradley's, Low Cock How, near Ennerdale Bridge. Tel: 01946 861354.

LONG-DISTANCE FOOTPATHS AND TRAILS

The Coast-to-Coast Walk
A 190-mile (304-km) walk from St Bees Head to Robin Hood's Bay in North Yorkshire.

The West Lakes Way
A 70-mile (112-km) walk from Whitehaven to Millom taking in Scafell, Pillar and Black Combe.

NATURE RESERVES

For details of the numerous coastal reserves contact the local Tourist Information Centres or Solway Rural Initiative.
Tel: 01693 22620.

SAILING

Crummock Water
Permits and boats for hire from Woodhouse, Buttermere.
Tel: 017687 70208.

Maryport
Maryport Marina. Tel: 01900 814431.

Annual Events and Customs

Broughton
Children's Carnival, early July.

Buttermere
Shepherds' Meet, mid-September.
Buttermere Show, early October.

Cockermouth
Cockermouth Sheepdog Trials, late May.
Cockermouth Carnival, late June.
Cockermouth Festival, throughout July.
Cockermouth and District Agricultural Show, late July.

Egremont
West Cumbria Rose Society Show, mid-July.
Crab Fair and the World Gurning Championship, mid-September.

Ennerdale Bridge
Ennerdale and Kinniside Agricultural Show, late August.

Lorton
Vale of Lorton Sheepdog Trials, late July.

Loweswater
Loweswater and Brackenthwaite Agricultural Show, mid-September.

Maryport
Maryport and District Carnival, early July.
Sea Shanty Festival, early August.

Whitehaven
Copeland Carnival, early July.

Workington
Curwen Fair, late May.

These checklists give details of just some of the facilities within the area covered by this guide. Further information can be obtained from Tourist Information Centres.

Bassenthwaite and Borrowdale

Keswick, a centre for walkers and holiday-makers alike, is the heart of the northern half of the Lake District, and it is certainly close to its geographical centre. The area around it also epitomises Lakeland scenery. To the south are the heavily wooded surrounds of Derwent Water which lead to the narrow pass known as the Jaws of Borrowdale, and the land here is harsh volcanic rock. To the north is the great hulk of Skiddaw, built up on smoother, softer slate. Further north still is lower-lying pasture land, where the River Wampool flows down to the Solway Firth with Scotland across the water.

BASSENTHWAITE LAKE Map ref NY2026
Owned by the National Park, only quiet activities are permitted on the lake. It is important as a home for a rare fish, the vendace, as well as for wintering wildfowl, and is designated as a Site of Special Scientific Interest and a National Nature Reserve. Bassenthwaite village is to the northeast, a short distance from the lake.

Beside the A591 are the grounds of 17th-century Mirehouse which lead down to the eastern shores of the lake and incorporate adventure playgrounds and a tea room set in the former sawmill. Near by is the Norman Church of St Bega. It is an inspiring setting, with Skiddaw (3,054 feet/931m) rising in the east. The location by the lake certainly inspired Tennyson, a regular visitor, who described, in *Morte d'Arthur*, the dying King Arthur being carried across the waters of the lake on a barge, thus making Bassenthwaite Lake the last resting place of Excalibur. A waymarked walk in the grounds allows visitors to enjoy the lakeside scenery, and to watch for swords rising out of the water!

Mirehouse has been in the same family since 1688. It has a wildflower meadow and a walled garden, while inside is a fine collection of furniture, literary portraits and manuscripts reflecting the family friendships with Tennyson, artist Francis Bacon, Scottish historian and essayist Thomas Carlyle and Edward Fitzgerald, English poet and translator of *The Rubáiyát of Omar Khayyám*.

LITERARY VISITORS

Thomas Carlyle was one of the many literary visitors to Mirehouse, though his description of the Lakeland poet, Samuel Taylor Coleridge, is less than flattering: 'He has no resolution, he shrinks from pain or labour in any of its shapes. His very attitude bespeaks this: he never straightens his knee joints, he stoops with his fat ill-shapen shoulders, and in walking he does not tread but shovel and slide.'

BORROWDALE GOWK

The tale is told that the people of Borrowdale were once called Borrowdale Gowk by outsiders, gowk being a local Cumbrian word for the cuckoo. Having caught a cuckoo at one time, the Borrowdale people thought that if they could keep it then it would remain spring all year round. They built a wall round the bird, but neglected to put a top on, so it escaped. There appear to be several holes in the logic of the story, too!

BORROWDALE Map ref NY2414

This glorious wooded valley which runs south from Derwent Water contains two of the Lake District's most dramatic natural features – the Bowder Stone and the Jaws of Borrowdale. The Stone is signposted along a path east of the B5289 Borrowdale road, south of the village of Grange. Why stop to look at a stone? Well this one weighs about 2,000 tons and appears to be balanced, ready to topple over. A set of steps leads up to the top of its 36 feet (11m), and despite the attempts of almost everyone who visits to give it a push, it hasn't fallen yet. It was put into place by a glacier, which later melted around it.

Here, too, are the so-called Jaws of Borrowdale, where the high crags on either side of the valley almost meet, squeezing the road and the river (the B5289 and the River Derwent) together as they both try to get through. Both do, and the road then swings round to the west, through the village of Seatoller, to climb through the equally dramatic Honister Pass, linking Borrowdale with Buttermere.

DERWENT WATER Map ref NY2519

South from Keswick spreads Derwent Water, it is the widest lake at 1¼ miles (2km) and is attractively dotted with islands. These include, in the very centre, St Herbert's Island, named for the saint who lived there as a hermit. There is also Derwent Isle, once home to German miners who worked around Keswick and in the

Derwent Water's four islands distinguish it from other lakes in the region

A silver birch cascades with autumn colour above the shores of Derwent Water

RED SQUIRRELS
These delightful little animals are found throughout the Lake District where mixed woodland provides an ideal habitat. In recent years their American cousin, the grey squirrel, has been advancing into the area from the south and possibly as a result of a virus it carries, causing a decline in the population of the red squirrel. Research and conservation measures are actively addressing the issue.

Newlands valley. With Borrowdale closing in to the south, and crags on either side of the lake's southern half, Derwent Water is a popular favourite. Popular too is the way in which it can be explored by using the ferries which ply between the seven landing stages around the lake, allowing visitors to get off and walk the many footpaths through the surrounding woods and up to the various excellent viewpoints. There are also good views from the high narrow road on the lake's western edge.

The eastern side is rich in waterfalls, such as the spectacular Lodore Falls in the southeastern corner, which is one of the stops for the ferries. Much of the land here is owned by the National Trust. This is largely due to the efforts of Canon Hardwicke Rawnsley, vicar of Crosthwaite, the parish church of Keswick. He was Secretary of the National Trust from its formation until his death in 1920. The beautiful Friar's Crag, on the northern shore of Derwent Water close to the Keswick boat landings, was purchased for the National Trust by public subscription to be his memorial. The view from here was deemed by Ruskin 'to be one of the finest in Europe'.

A LETTER FROM JOHN KEATS
In a letter to his brother and sister-in-law, George and Georgiana Keats, John Keats wrote on 28th June 1818: 'The Approach to Derwent Water is rich and magnificent beyond any means of conception – the Mountains all round sublime and graceful and rich in colour – Woods and wooded islands here and there – at the same time in the distance among Mountains of another aspect we see Basenthwaite – I shall drop like a Hawk on the Post Office at Carlisle to ask for some Letters from you and Tom.'

The tall tower of the 19th-century Moot Hall dominates Keswick's central square – note the single-handed clock

CASTLERIGG STONE CIRCLE
Two miles (3.2km) east of Keswick is one of the most dramatic and atmospheric stone circles in Britain (see Walk on page 80). It dates from about 2,000 BC, but its purpose remains unknown, adding to its enigmatic qualities. The 38 stones in the circle itself, with a further ten set in the centre, are surrounded by high fells, with Helvellyn to the southeast. They are made of volcanic Borrowdale rock, brought here by the glaciers of the Ice Age. The construction is actually oval in shape, 107 feet (33m) across at its widest point, and the name means 'the fort on the ridge', though no evidence of any fort exists here. Castlerigg Stone Circle is in the hands of the National Trust.

KESWICK Map ref NY2623

If Kendal is the main town in the southern Lakes, then Keswick is the heart of the north. It may not have Mint Cake but it has much else besides, as it is a natural centre for mountain climbers, country walkers and more leisurely tourists alike. It is small, with a population of under 5,000, but is said, for its size, to have more beds for visitors than anywhere else in the country. This gives an idea of what it can be like on a sunny August Bank Holiday Monday. No wandering lonely as a cloud down Keswick's busy streets.

If now reliant on tourism, in the past it was mining which kept Keswick alive. The industry flourished in the 16th century with the formation, by Elizabeth I and businesses with mining interests, of the Company of Mines Royal. Expert miners came from Germany and made their headquarters and home on Derwent Isle. There are still a few German surnames around today. At that time there were at least 20 mines, producing graphite, copper, iron, lead and some silver and gold. Large tracts of forest were cleared to fuel the smelting operations, but as the last mine closed in the 19th century, so opened the Cockermouth–Penrith railway line in 1865 to bring in the first of the visitors.

Graphite is the reason the Cumberland Pencil Museum exists here today. It is one of those delightfully quirky specialist collections which shows that even the humble pencil has a fascinating history. The first was made locally in the 1550s, though you can see modern production methods too (it's also a functioning factory), and the largest pencil in the world! An entertaining video includes a clip from the animated film *The Snowman*, drawn by artist Raymond Briggs using Cumberland pencils.

The Cars of the Stars Motor Museum is a fascinating collection started by a local dentist. Not all the cars have been used by the stars, however. Some are merely interesting vehicles, such as a curious Fiat from 1972 painted to look like its nickname – the Noddy Car. The 'Star Cars' range from one of the Reliant Robins used in the television series *Only Fools and Horses* (the BBC is known to have used several different vehicles for filming), to the Morris 8 Tourer driven by James Herriot in *All Creatures Great and Small*, and a selection of cars used in the James Bond films.

One of the oldest museums in the county is the Keswick Museum and Art Gallery which has a good display on Lakeland's literary connections. This covers in particular the poet Robert Southey, who moved to Greta Hall in Keswick (now part of a school) to join his brother-in-law, Coleridge, and remained there for over 40 years until his death in 1843. He became Poet Laureate in 1813. There is also a fine period scale model of the Lake District as it was in the early 19th century and, even older, a 500-year-old mummified cat! The comprehensive geology collection is of national importance and contains magnificent mineral examples from the Caldbeck Fells.

On the northern edge of Keswick at Crosthwaite is the Church of St Kentigern, whose best known incumbant, Canon Rawnsley, was the first secretary of the National Trust. A friend of Beatrix Potter, he was also an author, journalist, educationalist and orator. His influence pervades almost every corner of Keswick and Cumbria.

BEAR POET

Robert Southey (1774–1843) is perhaps the least known today of the Lakeland poets, despite the fact that he was Poet Laureate for 30 years. One of his works, however, has become such a well-known story that it is often believed to be a traditional fairy-tale. Not so. Robert Southey wrote the original version of *The Three Bears*, although the character of Goldilocks was a later embellishment by someone else.

The stones of the ancient circle at Castlerigg are weathered smooth, and spotted with golden lichen

Friar's Crag and Castlerigg Stone Circle

A splendid walk through some beautiful and varied landscapes and incorporating one of the best examples of a prehistoric stone circle in Britain. A few unchallenging climbs will take you into some of the most historic scenery in the Lake District.

Time: 3½–4 hours. Distance: 7 miles (11.3km).
Location: Just south of Keswick town centre.
Start: Car park on the edge of Derwent Water, off the B5289 south of Keswick. (OS grid ref: NY265229.)
OS Map: Outdoor Leisure 4
(The English Lakes – North Western area)
1:25,000.
See Key to Walks on page 121.

ROUTE DIRECTIONS

Take the lakeside road past the **Derwent Water** landing stages, go along the tree-lined track to the end of Friar's Crag for a view of the lake. Retrace your steps to follow a path that swings right to a gate and proceed along the lake shore. Cross two footbridges, then go through a gate into a wood. Continue along the woodland fringe, cross a footbridge, then bear right and go through a gate. Turn left along a metalled road. Shortly before reaching the Borrowdale road, turn right along a path through trees.

Continue for about 380 yards (350m) parallel to the road then, at the end of the fence, bear right into the wood. Go over the first of the two wooden bridges and turn left up to the road. Cross into Great Wood car park. Take the path from its right corner and climb gently for about 300 yards (274m) to a track which comes down on your left. Turn up this and continue for half a mile (0.8km) uphill through woodland. The path begins to level out and soon bear right at a junction, signed 'Rakefoot and Walla Crag'. Shortly the path ascends to a stile.

Go over the stile, leave the woodland and go ahead between a wall and a fence. At a T-junction turn right through a gate signed 'Castlerigg, Walla Crag'. Continue along the edge of the ravine and through another gate. Keep ahead and after 100 yards (91.5m) cross a footbridge on the left and keep ahead up steps, through a gate and turn left on to a metalled track. After 20 yards (18m) turn right through a gate signed 'Castlerigg Stone Circle'. Keep ahead on the left-hand edge of the field between a wall and a fence. Cross two stiles, turn left at the second stile following the sign for the stone circle. Follow the left-hand edge of the field crossing further stiles to reach a gate and the A591 Keswick to Windermere road. Turn right, then take the first left on to a track passing houses (High Nest). Keep ahead through a field gate then across stiles and fields to a lane next to a wood. Turn left on to a road; **Castlerigg Stone Circle** is in a field on your left.

From Friar's Crag you can see across to Causey Pike, rising sharply behind the trees on the opposite shore of the lake

After taking a break to view the stones and surrounding peaks, keep your back to the entrance gate and cross the field to the right to a stile, by a wall and fence junction, on to a lane. Turn left and continue for half a mile (0.8km) back to the A591. Turn right along the footpath beside this often busy road. After half a mile (0.8km), take the minor road left signed 'Rakefoot'. Beyond a house on the right, turn right through a gate (fingerpost) and follow a path that goes under a footbridge heading downhill through woodland to Brockle Beck.

Cross a footbridge, turn right and follow the stream downhill to a gate. Continue past Springs Farm, cross a bridge along a surfaced lane leading into Springs Road. After half a mile (0.8km), passing houses on the way, bear left down a narrow path to a gate. Ascend steps, continue uphill bearing right through dense woodland. Towards the top, climb steeply left to the fine viewpoint of Castlehead. Return through the trees, bearing left to the lower slopes of the hill, to join up with a path that descends to the left to steps at a gap in the wall and the B5289. Cross over and bear left to steps and a ramp on the right. Descend steps, then keep to the path ahead to reach a wood. Turn right to return to the car park.

POINTS OF INTEREST

Derwent Water

Typical of everything that is beautiful in the Lake District, this broad lake is ringed by mountain peaks and dotted with mysterious little tree-clad islands. It is best appreciated from the lofty Friar's Crag Viewpoint, south of the Keswick boat landings, which was said, by the writer John Ruskin, to be one of Europe's best scenic viewpoints.

Castlerigg Stone Circle

Dating from the late Neolithic/early Bronze Age *c*2,000–2,500 BC Castlerigg is one of the most imposing prehistoric monuments and probably the most spectacularly sited stone circle in the whole of Britain. At sunset on the summer solstice the tallest stone casts a long shadow.

JOHN PEEL

Parkend near Caldbeck, to the north of Skiddaw, is reputed to be the birthplace of John Peel. He was born in 1776 and did indeed become a renowned huntsman, not to mention a renowned drinker who neglected his family for his love of the hunt. The words to the song 'De Ye Ken John Peel' by which he was immortalised were written in 1832 by a friend, John Woodcock Graves, at his home in Caldbeck (a plaque adorns his house). Graves was a woollen manufacturer who also supplied the material for Peel's 'coat so grey'. Peel died in 1854, after a hunting accident. His grave can be seen in Caldbeck churchyard.

NEWLANDS Map ref NY2420

In the delightful Newlands valley, with its rolling green fields, there is little evidence left today that this was once a mining community. In fact you have to search hard to find communities at all, as there are only a handful of farms and the two tiny hamlets of Little Town and Stair. Having found them, each will stake its own claim to fame. A farmhouse at Stair has the inscription 'TF 1647'. The initials are believed to be those of Thomas Fairfax, commander of the Parliamentary forces, who stayed here during the turmoil following the end of the Civil War in 1646. Little Town's fame could hardly be more different as its name features in in Beatrix Potter's *The Tale of Mrs Tiggywinkle.*

Copper and lead were mined on the valley's eastern slopes, and small amounts of silver and gold were also found. The mines were developed by Elizabeth I, and miners were brought from Germany to help establish them. Today the landscape has returned to nature, a beautiful and gentle landscape down in the valley, but rising up through a steep and rugged pass in the southwest before descending to Buttermere.

SKIDDAW Map ref NY2629

When the Lakes first began to attract tourists in numbers in the 19th century, it was to Keswick that many of them came, and the one peak they would all walk to was Skiddaw. It is not the most attractive ascent lower down, but even though it rises to 3,054 feet (931m) it is a safe and easily manageable climb of little over two hours. You can even avoid the first 1,000 feet (305m) by parking at grid reference NY281254 above the village of Applethwaite, north of Keswick off the A591, and start

The bulky form of Skiddaw was a magnet to early fell-walkers

the climb there. In both places the path to Skiddaw is clearly signposted. At busy times of the year walkers will be going up in droves, so this is not a walk for those seeking solitude.

The rewards are at the top, however, even if you do have to share them with others. To the north are the mountains of Scotland, and in the far west is the Isle of Man. The peaks of the Pennines rise towards the east, while all around are Lakeland's other hills and dales. If your wish is to escape the crowds then take, instead, the Cumbria Way, which circles behind the main peak into the area known as 'Back o' Skiddaw'.

THIRLMERE Map ref NY3116

The A591 runs along the eastern side of the long thin lake of Thirlmere, with a car park near Wythburn chapel at the southern end. From here a track leads up to Helvellyn, and before 1879 many a path would have led downwards, too. For the chapel is all that remains of Wythburn village, flooded in the 19th century when Thirlmere was dammed at the northern end and turned into Manchester's first Lakeland reservoir. Armboth in the northwest is also now beneath the waters, along with several farms on the shores of the original lake.

Thirlmere, an attractive, tree-fringed expanse, is one of the few lakes that can be driven, as well as walked, around. A minor road runs down the western edge, a lovely drive through the lakeside woods with several car parks, each with forest trails leading off from them. One leads north up to Raven Crag, and good views are also to be had halfway down the western edge at Hause Point, where the lake was once narrow enough to have had a bridge across to the other side.

A traditional wooden sailing boat catches the breeze on Thirlmere

ONLY HALF WAY UP

Charles Brown, friend and biographer of the poet John Keats, accompanied him in 1818 on a walking tour through northern England, Scotland and Ireland. In his journal Brown wrote of their climb up Skiddaw from Keswick, and this extract shows that walking up mountains is the same for everyone: 'A promising morning authorised a guide to call us up at four o'clock, in order to ascend Skiddaw. The distance to the summit from the town is a little more than six miles. Its height, from the level of the sea, is 3,022 feet; but only 1,952 feet above Derwent Water – so lofty is all this part of the country. Helvellyn and Skawfell are somewhat higher, but the view from Skiddaw is esteemed the best. In a short time the continued steep became fatiguing; and then, while looking upward to what I thought was no very great distance from the top, it sounded like cruelty to hear from our guide that we were exactly half way!'

Bassenthwaite and Borrowdale

Checklist

Leisure Information
Places of Interest
Shopping
The Performing Arts
Sports, Activities and the Outdoors
Annual Events and Customs

Leisure Information

TOURIST INFORMATION CENTRES

Borrowdale
Seatoller Barn. Tel: 017687 77294.

Keswick
Moot Hall, Market Square. Tel: 017687 72645.

Silloth
10 Criffel Street. Tel: 016973 31944.

OTHER INFORMATION

Cumbria Wildlife Trust
Brockhole, Windermere. Tel: 015394 48280.

English Heritage
Canada House, 3 Chepstow St, Manchester. Tel: 0161 242 1400. www.english-heritage.org.uk

Lake District National Park Authority Headquarters
Murley Moss, Oxenholme Road, Kendal. Tel: 01539 724555. www.lake-district.gov.uk

National Trust in Cumbria
The Hollens, Grasmere, Ambleside, Cumbria. Tel: 015394 35599. www.nationaltrust.org.uk

Public Transport
The Traveline service gives details of buses, boats, trains and ferries operating throughout Cumbria. Tel: 0870 608 2608.

Weather
Lake District Weather Service. Tel: 017687 75757.

ORDNANCE SURVEY MAPS

Landranger 1:50,000 Sheets 85, 89.
Outdoor Leisure 1:25,000 Sheet 4.

Places of Interest

There will be an admission charge at the following places of interest unless otherwise stated.

Cars of the Stars Motor Museum
Standish Street, Keswick. Tel: 017687 73757. Vehicles from television and film displayed in authentic settings. Open Easter–New Year, daily.

Castlerigg Stone Circle
2 miles (3.2km) east of Keswick. Open all year. Free.

Cumberland Pencil Museum
Southey Works, Carding Mill Lane, Keswick. Tel: 017687 73626. Displays of the history of the pencil, an entertaining video, and modern production methods. Open all year, daily except Christmas and New Year's Day.

Honister Slate Mine
Honister Pass. Tel: 017687 77230. Working mine offers underground tours. Open all year, most days.

Keswick Museum and Art Gallery
Fitz Park, Station Road, Keswick. Tel: 017687 73263. Literary displays include letters and manuscripts; also geology and natural history of the area. Open Easter–Oct, daily.

Mining and Quarrying Museum
Threlkeld, near Keswick. Tel: 017687 79747. Exhibits in a former quarry complex illustrate all aspects of Cumbrian mining, quarrying and geology. Open Easter–Oct, daily and winter weekends.

Mirehouse
Three miles (4.6km) north of Keswick, off the A591. Tel: 017867 72287. Seventeenth-century house where Tennyson wrote *Morte d'Arthur*. Walled garden, lakeside walks, four adventure playgrounds. Open: house Apr–Oct certain days; grounds open all year, daily.

The Teapottery
Central Car Park Road, Keswick. Tel: 017687 73983. Watch handmade collectable teapots being made, learn of the history of tea and browse in the shop.

SPECIAL INTEREST FOR CHILDREN

The following places may be of interest to visitors with children. Unless otherwise stated, there will be an admission charge.

Cars of the Stars Motor Museum
Standish Street, Keswick. Tel: 017687 73757. Vehicles from television and film displayed in authentic settings. Open Easter–New Year, daily.

Cumberland Pencil Museum
Southey Works, Carding Mill Lane, Keswick. Tel: 017687 73626. Displays of the history of the pencil, video and modern production methods. Open all year, daily except Christmas and New Year's Day.

Mirehouse
Three miles (4.8km) north of Keswick, off the A591. Tel: 017867 74317. Seventeenth-century house where Tennyson wrote *Morte d'Arthur*. Walled garden, adventure playgrounds. Open: house Apr–Oct, certain days; grounds open all year, daily.

Shopping

Keswick
Market, Sat.

LOCAL SPECIALITIES

Silloth Shrimps
Available from local fishmongers.

Solway Firth Salmon
Available from local fishmongers.

Sweet Cumberland Ham
Available from local butchers.

The Performing Arts

Theatre by the Lake
Lakeside, Keswick. Tel: 017687 74411.

Sports, Activities and the Outdoors

ANGLING

Bassenthwaite Lake
Permits from Blencathra Centre, Threlkeld. Tel: 017687 79633. Swan Hotel, Thornthwaite. Tel: 017687 78256.

Derwent Water
Permits from Field and Stream, 79 Main Street, Keswick. Tel: 017687 74396.

BOAT HIRE

Derwent Water
Derwent Water Marina, Portinscale. Tel: 017687 72912.
Keswick Launch. Tel: 017687 72263.
Nichol End Marine, Portinscale. Tel: 017687 73082.

BOAT TRIPS

Derwent Water
Regular passenger service calling at various landing stages on the lake. Keswick Launch. Tel: 017687 72263.

CYCLE HIRE

Keswick
Keswick Motor Co, Lake Road. Tel: 017687 72064.
Keswick Mountain Bike Centre, Southey Hill Estate. Tel: 017687 75202.
Lakeland Pedlar, Bell Close Car Park. Tel: 017687 75752.

GOLF COURSES

Aspatria
Brayton Park Golf Club, Brayton Park. Tel: 016973 20840.

Cockermouth
Cockermouth Golf Club, Embleton. Tel: 017687 76223.

Keswick
Keswick Golf Club, Threlkeld Hall. Tel: 017687 79324.

Silloth
Silloth-on-Solway Golf Club, The Clubhouse. Tel: 016973 31304.

HORSE-RIDING

Bassenthwaite
Armathwaite Hall Equestrian Centre, Coal Beck Farm. Tel: 017687 76949.

Silloth
Stanwix Park Holiday Centre. Tel: 016973 32861.

Troutbeck
Rookin House Farm. Tel: 017684 83561.

The old church beside Bassenthwaite Lake, dedicated to St Bega, was a favourite haunt of Tennyson

Roses flourish against a cottage wall in a sunny corner of Thornthwaite, near Keswick

LONG-DISTANCE FOOTPATHS AND TRAILS

The Allerdale Ramble
A 55-mile (88-km) walk from the Borrowdale valley to Silloth.

The Cumbria Coastal Way
A 124-mile (198.4-km) walk from Barrow-in-Furness to Carlisle.

SAILING

Bassenthwaite
Bassenthwaite Sailing Club.
Tel: 017687 76341.

Derwent Water
Derwent Water Marina.
Tel: 017687 72912.
Platty Plus, Lodore Boat Landing.
Tel: 017687 76572.
Nichol End Marine. Tel: 017687 73082.

WATERSPORTS

Derwent Water
Derwent Water Marina, Portinscale. Tel: 017687 72912.
Canoeing and windsurfing are available.
Nichol End Marine.
Tel: 017687 73082.
Platty Plus, Lodore Boat Landing.
Canoeing and windsurfing are available.
Tel: 017687 76572.

Annual Events and Customs

Bassenthwaite
Bassenthwaite Sailing Week, early August.

Borrowdale
Borrowdale Shepherds' Meet and Show, mid-September.

Caldbeck
Caldbeck and Hesket Newmarket Sheepdog Trials, late August.
Hesket Newmarket Show, early September.

Cockermouth
Agricultural Show, late July.

Keswick
Keswick Jazz Festival, mid-May.
Carnival, mid-June.
Keswick Convention, mid to late July.
Keswick Victorian Fair, early December.

Silloth
Kite Festival, mid-July.
Silloth Carnival, August Bank Holiday Monday.
Trawler Race, early August.

Threlkeld
Threlkeld Sheepdog Trials, mid-August.

Uldale
Uldale Village Show, early September.
Uldale Shepherds' Meet and Blencathra Hunt, early December.

These checklists give details of just some of the facilities within the area covered by this guide. Further information can be obtained from Tourist Information Centres.

Ullswater, Penrith and the Eastern Fells

This is a very varied corner of the Lake District. To the south and west is what we expect from the area: expanses of water such as Haweswater and Ullswater, surrounded by soaring mountains like Helvellyn. Head further east, however, and you move through the more rolling green Eden Valley, beyond which stand the rugged Pennine mountains. There are market towns and ancient monuments, border towns and their castles, stately homes and gardens – and also fewer of the crowds drawn to the central and southern Lakes. In short, there is much to see, and plenty of room to see it in.

ALSTON Map ref NY7146

Alston would be one of the prettiest market towns in England, but for one thing – it no longer has a market. High in the northern Pennines, it still has its market cross, and a reputation for local delicacies such as Alston cheese and Alston mustard. The town was built around the lead-mining industry on Alston Moor, and although that industry has now gone visitors can still go prospecting for lead at Nenthead, 5 miles (8km) southeast of the town. From Alston, the narrow-gauge South Tynedale Railway uses steam and diesel engines to take visitors on trips along this very attractive valley.

NENTHEAD

Nenthead Mines Heritage Centre tells the story of how the Quaker London Lead Company has left a remarkable social and economic legacy in the north Pennines. The centre, the mines and the village evoke a vivid reminder of past life and work in this remote upland landscape.

The sign at Alston says it all

There are extensive views to the Pennine hills from the parapet of Appleby Castle

EAST CUMBRIA COUNTRYSIDE PROJECT

This organisation sponsors an award-winning programme of guided and self-guided walks and tours throughout the Eden Valley and the north Pennine area of east Cumbria. It has also promoted Eden Benchmarks, a series of ten imaginative sculptures on paths beside the River Eden between its source in Mallerstang and its mouth at Rockcliffe. Details are available from local Tourist Information Centres.

APPLEBY-IN-WESTMORLAND Map ref NY6820

Appleby has a great deal to commend it, including its setting, in a loop of the tree-lined River Eden, above which its Norman castle stands protectively. Appleby Castle has an impressive 11th-century keep, although a lot of the building dates from the 17th century when it was restored by the redoubtable Lady Anne Clifford. The present owners have turned the grounds into an admirable Conservation Centre.

Appleby was once the county town of Westmorland, with a royal charter dating from 1174. At either end of its main street, Boroughgate, the High Cross and the Low Cross mark what were the boundaries of Appleby market. The attractive almshouses known as Lady Anne's Hospital are still maintained by a trust fund set up by Lady Anne Clifford to provide accommodation for 13 poor widows from the castle estate. Lady Anne, whose mark was felt all over the Lake District and the Yorkshire Dales, is buried here in Appleby, her tomb lying in St Lawrence's Church, which can also boast one of the oldest surviving working church organs in the country. Another boast is that among the former pupils of the town's Grammar School were the brothers of the first American president, George Washington.

The village of Morland, 7 miles (11.2km) northwest of Appleby, has won several Best Kept Village awards, and the village church has an Anglo-Saxon tower, the oldest in Cumbria. Interesting features inside the church include the font dated 1662, 15th-century carved heads on a beam in front of the organ and a beautiful east window dating from 1920.

BAMPTON Map ref NY5118

Bampton is a place of doubles, it has two villages, two rivers, two bridges and two pubs. Firstly there is Bampton itself, then its neighbouring village of Bampton Grange. The two are separated only by a bridge across Haweswater Beck, which joins the River Lowther here in this charming wooded valley. Appropriately, the name of Bampton derives from two Old English words meaning 'the farmstead by a tree'. In Bampton Grange a second bridge, of sandstone, stands by St Patrick's Church which was built in 1726 on the site of an earlier church. It was restored in 1885, just eight years after the nearby Wesleyan Chapel was built. Inside is a picture of Mardale church, which was lost when Mardale village was 'drowned' by extending Haweswater reservoir. A few village houses have date stones over their doors, showing their 17th-century origins.

Bampton was once a more flourishing village, with several shops and those farmsteads which gave the village its name. Today there is a single village store which also doubles as the post office and café. The tourists stop off here on their way to Haweswater. Just before the reservoir is the village of Burnbanks, built to accommodate the families of those working on the reservoir for Manchester Corporation. Few of the original dwellings remain, but some have been converted for use as local or holiday homes.

THE MARDALE HUNT SHEPHERDS' MEET

This November institution at St Patrick's Well Inn, Bampton Grange, is one of several throughout Cumbria. Originally a time to reclaim stray sheep, it now centres around a fox hunt – which is followed on foot, as the terrain is unsuitable for horses. Afterwards a good time is had by all with the hunt supper, a drink or three, and the traditional hunting songs.

Dark-fleeced Herdwick sheep are a familiar sight in the area

THE VENERABLE BEDE

Bede was born in about the year AD 673 and became both a theologian and historian. His major work was published in AD 731 in Latin as *Historia Ecclesiastica Gentis Anglorum*, or the *Ecclesiastical History of the English Nation*. Bede was a Benedictine monk in the monastery at Jarrow at the time, and this work, which remains a major source for the history of the period AD 597–731, has been described as marking the start of English literature. It was also Bede who began dating events from the Birth of Christ. He died in AD 735, but did not become 'Venerable' until about a century later.

A set of mysterious stone carvings stands in the churchyard at Dacre

DACRE AND DALEMAIN Map ref NY4526/4627

There are layers of history and elements of mystery in the village of Dacre. The Norman church stands on the site of a Saxon monastery, and the 14th-century castle is known to have been built on the site of a much earlier fortification. The castle claims to have a ghost, although visitors will have to be content with local stories as the building is not open to the public unless prior arrangements have been made.

Dacre church is of great historical interest. Some features date from the 12th and 13th centuries, while in the churchyard are four mysterious stones whose origins are completely unknown. Each depicts a bear. One is asleep, one being attacked by a cat, the third grabbing the cat and the fourth bear eating it. Visitors must draw their own conclusions as to their meaning. The stones may date back to the monastery, whose existence is mentioned by the Venerable Bede in AD 731, while a later reference shows that the 'Peace of Dacre' was signed in the village in 926 between Athelstan of England and Constantine of Scotland.

A minor road links Dacre castle with Dalemain, to the northeast of the village. This mix of medieval, Tudor, Georgian and a few other styles too, has been the home of the Hasell family since 1665, with guided tours available. Dalemain is very much a friendly family home rather than a formal stately home. It has Queen Anne and Georgian furniture, a Victorian nursery, several small museums, including a collection of old agricultural implements in a barn and an interesting display on the local fell ponies. Outside, a herd of fallow deer roam the deer park, and an adventure playground keeps children amused, if not necessarily quiet.

Leave your vehicle in the car park at Haweswater and take the circular footpath

HAWESWATER Map ref NY4713

It may sound like another of nature's lakes, but Haweswater is in fact a reservoir, created in the 1930s. Beneath its surface lies the village of Mardale and the one-time dairy farms of the Haweswater valley. The land was bought by Manchester Corporation who needed an extra reservoir – they were already using Thirlmere – to supply the needs of a booming industrial city. A 94-foot (28.7-m) dam was begun in 1929, the valley then flooded, trees were planted, and Haweswater today has a different kind of beauty.

Wildlife abounds in the area, with peregrine falcons, buzzards, sparrowhawks and even golden eagles now breeding in the valley. The eagles are closely monitored by the RSPB, but an observation post allows visitors to watch their activities from a distance. Otters have also colonised the area, no doubt feeding on the rare char and freshwater herring which are also found here. Other mammals include both roe and red deer, and red squirrels (see the side panel on page 77). Manchester Corporation may have drowned the houses of Mardale, but in doing so they created a new and very healthy wildlife community.

On the western shores of the reservoir steep crags rise to Bampton Common, while in the east is the ancient Naddle Forest, refuge of wood warblers, tree pipits, redstarts and several species of woodpecker. The path which winds through the woods is part of a circular walk all round Haweswater. This was finally made possible only in 1995, when the last four miles (6.4km) of footpath along the southern edge of the reservoir were completed to make one of the best circular walks in the Lake District.

MARDALE'S RETURN

Although Mardale village was lost when Haweswater was deepened, that was not the last that people had seen of it. During the summer drought of 1995, when water levels dropped, it appeared again, though not quite as much as it did in a similar drought in 1984. Then it was actually possible to walk round the village once more, and many of its old residents took the chance to look at their old homes again, some 50 years on.

CONSERVING CUMBRIA

Visitors can help the environment by parking their cars and using the waymarked walks, cycling, taking the local trains, buses, minibus tours, and launches on the lakes. During the summer an open-top bus service operates between Bowness, Windermere, Ambleside and Grasmere. The Coniston Rambler links Windermere, Ambleside, Hawkshead and Coniston and a service from Keswick leaves for Borrowdale and Buttermere. Minibus tours are a popular way of seeing the high passes; their main centres are Windermere and Keswick.

HELVELLYN Map ref NY3415

Wordsworth's favourite mountain is the favourite of countless thousands more, who regularly trek to its summit at 3,116 feet (950m). It is indeed a grand climb, but its popularity should not mask its difficulty, as it has its arduous stretches and on no account should a walk be undertaken if the weather forecast is bad. Mist can come down rapidly in these high fells, and deaths through exposure are not uncommon in the Lake District, and not only in the depths of winter.

Warnings aside, the peak is accessible by reasonably fit walkers, a popular approach being from Wythburn on the southeastern shores of Thirlmere reservoir. This takes the walker up Helvellyn's steep southwestern slopes, with splendid views of the Cumbrian Mountains across Thirlmere to the west. The eastern approaches are longer but scenically even more dramatic, from Grisedale or Glenridding, for example, but a detailed Ordnance Survey map will be needed.

The arduous climb may have taken your breath away, but the views from the top of Helvellyn will do so again – north along the valley towards Keswick, and east beyond the mountain lake, Red Tarn, to the distant high peaks of the Pennines. Just south of the summit is a memorial containing some words, not just by Wordsworth, but by Sir Walter Scott, too. The words are at least a sign that your endeavours have taken you to the highest point in the area for there are 6 miles (9.6km) of mountains here, with other peaks such as Lower Man and Great Dodd being only a few hundred feet less than Helvellyn itself. Only Scafell Pike, at 3,210 feet (978m), and Scafell, at 3162 feet (964m), are higher than Helvellyn.

Bright fireweed forms a foreground for this spectacular view of Helvellyn

The architecture of impressive Hutton-in-the-Forest owes much to the 19th-century 'improver' Anthony Salvin

HUTTON-IN-THE-FOREST Map ref NY4636

Hutton-in-the-Forest, 4 miles (6.4km) northwest of Penrith, sounds like a tucked-away fairy-tale village. In fact it is the stately home of the Vane family and has been since 1600. It was originally owned by the de Huttons on land they were granted in return for caring for the deer reserve, and for holding the king's stirrup whenever he mounted his horse in Carlisle Castle. The first building here was probably a pele tower built in the 14th century, while the rest of the house is a mix of styles from the 17th century onwards. Some of the older features include a Gallery dating from 1630s, and a grand 1680s Hall. It is said to have been the home of the Green Knight of the Arthurian poem 'Sir Gawain and the Green Knight', but today it is a delightfully low-key stately home, the residence of Lord Inglewood, the present head of the family.

The grounds are worth seeing, as the present owners take an active interest in their development, yet also allowing parts to remain wild. A particular treat is a walled garden which dates from the 1730s. Monthly 'Meet the Gardener' walks round the grounds offer a chance to hear the problems and pleasures of being responsible for a garden this size. It includes a wildflower meadow, and a lake where nature is largely allowed to take its course. There are streams and woodlands, and the mix of the planned and the natural is a delight.

THE GREEN KNIGHT

In the 14th-century poem, 'Sir Gawain and the Green Knight', a Green Knight enters Camelot during the New Year's celebrations and issues a challenge to Arthur's knights. He says that anyone may cut off his head provided they agree to have their own head cut off in one year's time. Sir Gawain cuts off the knight's head, only to see him pick it up and ride away. One year later he sets off to seek the knight to accept his fate. He reaches a beautiful castle (allegedly Hutton-in-the-Forest) where the story gets complicated, involving hunting, bargains, the inevitable amorous adventures, betrayal and girdles. Sir Gawain receives no more than a nick on the neck from the castle's owner, who was the Green Knight in disguise, and they all lived happily ever after.

The Shoemaker's Hill – Souther Fell

Not a difficult walk but it can be wet in parts. You will, however, be rewarded by lovely views, up and down the valley of fells to the south and to the west.

Time: 4–5 hours. Distance: 5 miles (8km).
Location: 10 miles (16km) northeast of Keswick.
Start: Mungrisdale village situated 2 miles (3.2km) off the A66 Keswick to Penrith road, from a junction one mile (1.6km) east of Scales. Park on the side of the road in, or near, the village and locate the Mill Inn. (OS grid ref: NY363303.)
OS Map: Outdoor Leisure 5
(The English Lakes – North Eastern area)
1:25,000.
See Key to Walks on page 121.

ROUTE DIRECTIONS

From the bridge by the Mill Inn in **Mungrisdale**, follow the lane towards the village, keep ahead at this point to visit the **church** in the north of the village, otherwise shortly turn left along a farm lane. To begin the walk around **Souther Fell**, continue past the farm on to an old mine track which runs parallel with the river. Soon the track bears to the left and descends. Cross a small footbridge and then take the minor path to the left just before the main track goes uphill. This minor track keeps parallel to, and above, the river.

Shortly you reach some wet and boggy sections. These can be avoided by going above them, or walking on the stony ground below them. The river you are following is the Glenderamackin, a Celtic name connected to the Welsh *Glyndwrmochyn*, meaning the 'river valley of the pig', which would link it, and Mungrisdale, to the Norse *gris dale*, which means 'pig valley'.

Continue on the path and shortly cross Bannerdale Beck coming down from the right. The path now gradually ascends, following the River Glenderamackin which is down to the left. After about one mile (1.6km) from Bannerdale Beck the path swings round to the right. Soon take a narrow path that forks left and descend to a footbridge over River Glenderamackin. Cross the bridge and follow the path up to the left to the top of Mousthwaite Comb. This is the highest point of the walk and gives excellent views south to Clough Head 2,381 feet (726m) and the **Helvellyn** range 3,116 feet (950m).

When you reach the top of Mousthwaite Comb go straight ahead on a level indistinct path and bear across to the right to meet a distinct path that bears to the right and leads down into Mousthwaite Comb. (Do not take the path that goes ahead round the left-hand rim of the Comb.)

Follow the stony path down towards the bottom of the Comb, cross a series of boardwalks and a stile by a sheepfold on the right. Join a metalled lane and turn left. Follow the lane for about 2 miles (3.2km). At Low Beckside keep left and follow the lane back to the inn and the start of the walk.

Take the time to stoke up before you set off, at the Mill Inn at Mungrisdale

POINTS OF INTEREST

Mungrisdale

The name Mungrisdale tells several stories. Firstly, Mungo was the name given to St Kentigern by those who were close to him, and comes from the Celtic *mwyn gu*, meaning 'my dear one'; the church here is dedicated to him. Kentigern is credited with founding both the church in Glasgow and possibly St Asaph's Cathedral in North Wales. *Gris dale* are the Norse words for 'pig valley'.

Mungrisdale Church

St Kentigern's Church may have been established here in AD 552 but the present church was rebuilt in 1756. It is a simple building that Kentigern would probably have been proud of. It contains a fine 17th-century triple-decker pulpit.

Souther Fell

Pronounced locally as 'sowter', this probably best approximates the Norse word for shoemaker. The fell is at the most southeasterly part of the Blencathra massif; the name comes from the Welsh for summit and chair. So Saddleback, as it is often called, is almost a direct translation.

Helvellyn

Helvellyn is the third highest peak in the Lake District. The dramatic glaciated scenery around the mountain has attracted artists and photographers since the earliest days of tourism.

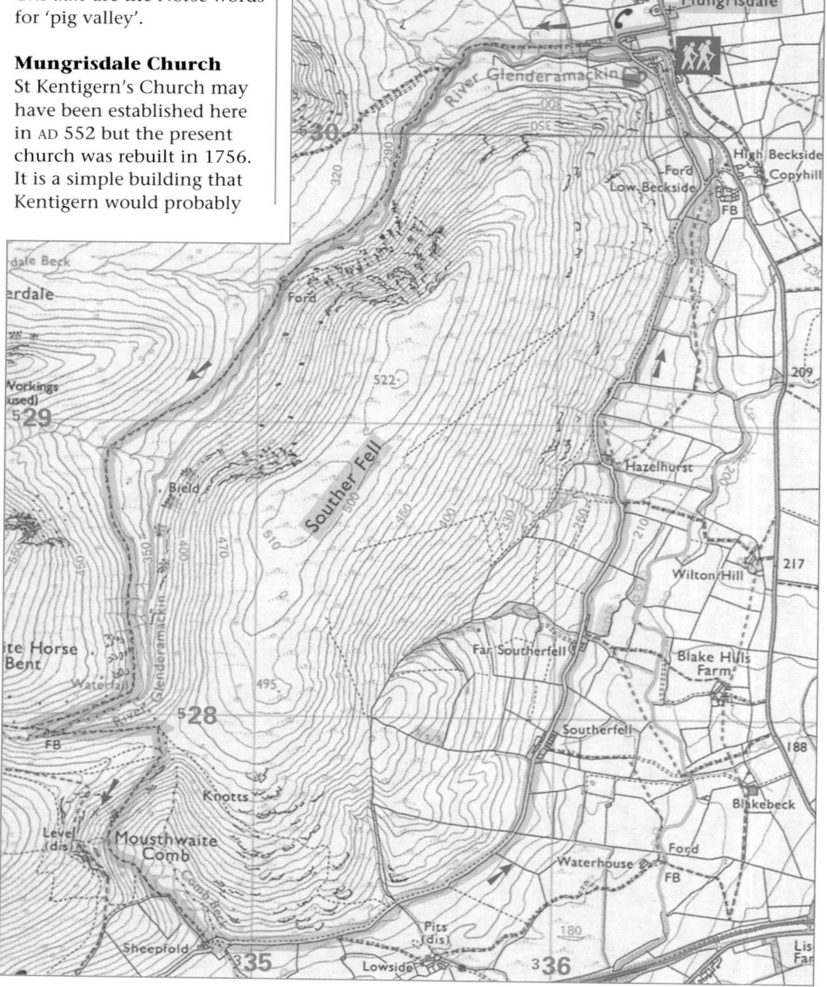

The shell of Lowther Castle, visible from the public road, is an extraordinary sight

THE 'YELLOW EARL'

In 1911 the 5th Earl of Lonsdale, Hugh Cecil Lowther, became the first President of the Automobile Association. He was known as the 'Yellow Earl' because that was his favourite colour, and it was a coincidence that the AA had already adopted yellow for its livery and still uses it in its logo today. The earl drove a yellow Rolls-Royce, and his influence was such that Cumbrian Conservatives also adopted yellow rather than the traditional blue as their colour. He was a great sportsman, and became President of the National Sporting Club; in that capacity, he initiated boxing's Lonsdale Belt – also yellow. The earl died in 1944 and is buried in Lowther churchyard.

LOWTHER Map ref NY5323

Lowther is an amalgamation of village, castle, estate and now a Leisure Park. They all stand, more or less together, just off the A6 and just inside the northeastern edge of the National Park. Lowther Castle is a rather splendid-looking illusion. It was built in 1806–11, but the upkeep proved to be too expensive and the inside was torn out, leaving today an empty shell (not open to the public). The 17th-century Church of St Michael on the estate can be visited, its graveyard contains the mausoleum to the 1st Earl of Lonsdale, who died in 1844 and to whom Wordsworth dedicated his 1814 work, 'The Excursion'.

For children tired of too much scenery and history, a day's visit to the 150-acre Lowther Leisure Park might have more appeal. With both open-air and wet-weather rides and entertainments, it is a place worth knowing about, as adults can also enjoy the surprisingly peaceful scenic walks among the herds of red deer.

PENRITH Map ref NY5130

In the 9th and 10th centuries Penrith was the capital of the Kingdom of Cumbria, incorporated into England in 1070. It was another of those border market towns which proved vulnerable to Scottish raiders, who sacked it several times in the 14th century. Penrith Beacon on Beacon Hill at the town's northern edge was lit to warn the inhabitants of impending raids, and today it makes a good viewpoint. The ruined red sandstone castle (English Heritage), which stands in Castle Park, dates from the early 15th century when attempts were made to strengthen and extend the fortifications.

There are many more buildings of architectural and historical interest. Penrith Museum is housed in a 1670 schoolhouse and St Andrew's Church dates from the 18th century; its graveyard contains the reputed grave of Caesarius, the giant 10th-century Cumbrian king – in fact these are 1,000-year-old 'hog-back' tombstones. It was in Devonshire Street that William and Dorothy Wordsworth stayed with their grandparents while they attended Dame Birkett's School, first built in 1563. In King Street is the plague stone, where food was left out for those who were stricken with the plague. The Cumbria Police Museum is in the Police Headquarters at Carleton Hall. Appointments need to be made to see the small but enjoyable collection, which includes the monocle worn by Percy Toplis, who achieved fame as the 'Monocled Mutineer'.

One mile (1.6km) south of Penrith at Eamont Bridge stands the circular Mayburgh Earthwork. Dating from prehistoric times, its 15-foot (4.5m) banks surround an area of roughly 1½ acres, inside which is a huge and solitary stone.

Wetheriggs Country Pottery, 4 miles (6.4km) south of Penrith, has been in existence since 1855 and the steam-powered pottery can still be toured. Several different craftspeople are likely to be working at any one time, and visitors can do what they always want to do at a pottery: try their hand at throwing the clay.

Also worth seeking out, in Melmerby 8 miles (12.8km) northeast of Penrith off the A686, is the award-winning Village Bakery. It is the only commercial bakery in England using wood-fired brick ovens. Here baker Andrew Whitley produces bread and cakes to traditional local recipes; Westmorland parkin, Grasmere gingerbread, Borrowdale tea bread and Cumberland rum nicky are just some of the treats on the menu of this shop, tea shop and restaurant.

RHEGED – UPLAND KINGDOM DISCOVERY CENTRE

This major new visitor facility, on the A66 just west of junction 40 of the M6, is named after the 5th- and 6th-century British kingdom of which Cumbria was a part. It interprets the history and life of the area through film and a range of innovative techniques. Rheged is also the home of the National Mountaineering Exhibition. Partly underground, yet looking out to the local environment, it has a range of catering facilities, shops and a tourist information centre.

Look out in Penrith for a fearsome pair of rampant boars, part of the crest above the door of the Gloucester Arms

SHAP AND KELD Map ref NY5615

Shap stone has been used in the making of many fine monuments, including the Albert Memorial and St Pancras Station in London, but the village's own monument is Shap Abbey, standing in a picturesque setting by the River Lowther. It was founded in 1199 by the Premonstratensian order also known as the White Canons from the colour of their habits. The west tower is the most imposing part of the remains, and this actually dates from about 1500, but there are sections of wall, too, and not a great deal of imagination is needed to conjure up a picture of monastic life here. After the Dissolution of the Monasteries, part of the area here was also used as a quarry, but the remote Abbey remains are now in the hands of English Heritage.

It is the National Trust who look after the 15th-century Keld Chapel, in the scattering of houses near by that make up the hamlet of Keld. The simple chapel is still used for occasional services today, but is normally locked, though instructions for obtaining the key are pinned to the chapel door.

Evidence of Neolithic and Bronze-Age settlements have been found around both these villages, but most of the standing stones which existed have been removed, and a stone circle near Shap was destroyed when the railway was built. The Goggleby Stone stands by a footpath leading from Shap to Keld, while the Thunder Stone is half a mile (0.8km) to the northwest, off the road to Rosgill.

EXCESS 'S'

Keld is the Norse name for a well or a spring, and is more typical of names found slightly further south and east, along Yorkshire's Swaledale. Indeed, there is another village called Keld in Swaledale itself. The name Shap, however, derives from the Old English and is the same root as our modern word heap. It is possible that an old stone circle may have been here, the village growing up with the name of Heap, for 'heap of stones', with the initial 's' being added later.

The ruins of Shap Abbey lie to the west of the village

Enjoying the spring sunshine in the gardens at Acorn Bank

TEMPLE SOWERBY Map ref NY6127

For those who want to see a true host of golden daffodils in the Lake District, then one of the finest spring displays is at Acorn Bank Garden at Temple Sowerby. Whole swathes of yellow bob in the wind beneath the grand oak trees which form an important part of these 2½ acres, owned by the National Trust. Acorn Bank is particularly noted for its walled herb garden, which contains the largest collection of medicinal, culinary and even narcotic herbs in the north of England; in all some 250 species. Some are poisonous, so you are warned not to try nibbling them! There are traditional orchards, too, and fine collections of roses, shrubs and herbaceous borders. Gardeners can stock up with plants from the small shop.

The garden is not just of interest to gardeners, though. A circular woodland walk has been created, which makes for a pleasant stroll as it takes the visitor for part of the way through woods alongside Crowdundle Beck and to the restored watermill.

It is the gardens here which originally provided the name for the nearby village of Temple Sowerby. It is known that as long ago as 1228 the Knights Templar had a religious house on this spot, but the oldest parts of the present buildings date back to the 16th century. Nor is the herb garden an ancient one, it was begun by the National Trust who took over the gardens in 1969.

KNIGHTS TEMPLAR

The origins of the Knights Templar go back to 1119 in Jerusalem, when two French knights set up an organisation to protect pilgrims visiting Palestine after the First Crusade. The name comes from Solomon's Temple, their first headquarters in Jerusalem. The Knights became very powerful throughout Europe, developing one of the first effective banking systems, but their power was so strong that they were suppressed by Pope Clement V in 1312 when their Grand Master and many leading officers were burnt at the stake after confessing (under torture) to crimes of sacrilege and devil-worship. They were subsequently disbanded in England on the orders of Edward II, but still exist today as Freemasons.

ULFR

Ullswater sounds an unusual word but it is quite a straightforward one, meaning the lake of Ulfr. Who this particular Ulfr was is uncertain, but it was a common enough Old Norse name. Ulverston is Ulfr's farmstead. The name also means a wolf, and so names such as Uldale, Ullock, Ulpha and Ullthwaite all have lupine connections.

ULLSWATER Map ref NY4220

On the western shores of Ullswater, a series of splendid waterfalls tumbles down through the wooded gorge of Aira Beck which flows into the region's second largest lake, some 7½ miles (12km) long. The falls are known by the name of the largest, the 70-foot (21.3-m) drop of Aira Force (see Walk on page 102), on land owned by the National Trust. Here too is an arboretum, café and a landscaped Victorian park.

Back in 1802, the falls did not just feed the waters of Ullswater, they fed, as well, the imagination of William and Dorothy Wordsworth. The poet and his sister were walking near by on 15th April, perhaps in the adjacent woods of Gowbarrow Park, although scholars argue this point, but it was Dorothy who observed the 'daffodils so beautiful... they tossed and reeled and danced.' The words and thoughts were transformed by her brother into one of the best-known and best-loved of English poems – 'Daffodils' ('I wandered lonely as a cloud...'). Aira Force itself is also the setting for another poem, 'The Somnambulist'.

It is appropriate that the poet was inspired by what, for many people, is the lake among lakes, indisputably beautiful. The southern tip of its slim shape is below the shoulders of Helvellyn (3,116 feet/950m), to the west, and reached through the dramatic and high Kirkstone Pass, which rises to 1,489 feet (454m). Near here is the Kirkstone Pass Inn, third highest pub in the country. Look, too, for the rock which is said to resemble a

Undoubtedly one of the loveliest of the lakes, Ullswater curves towards Glenridding

Take to the lake on one of the elegant old craft which ply these blue waters

church steeple and which gives the pass its name – church-stone.

At Pooley Bridge on the lake's northern tip, a fish market used to be held in the main square, and this area is still rich in trout and salmon. A short walk up to Dunmallard Hill reveals Iron-Age remains and lovely views. Below here at the pier near the 16th-century bridge, two 19th-century steamers leave to take visitors down the lake. The two ships, *Lady of the Lake* and *Raven*, date from 1877 and 1889 respectively, an indication of how long visitors have been enjoying these waters.

The steamers call at Howtown, roughly halfway down Ullswater's eastern shore, then travel on to Glenridding at the southern end. A popular option is to combine a cruise with a walk, and no finer walk is said to exist in the Lakes than that between Howtown and Glenridding. For much of the way the footpath skirts Ullswater's shores, with magnificent views across the waters and Helvellyn rising beyond. There is no road through this steep-cliffed southeastern shore of the lake. The cruise boat could then be rejoined at Glenridding, but don't let the distances deceive you. The lake may be only 7½ miles (12km) long, but that is also roughly the distance by foot from Howtown to Glenridding. The curve of its crescent shape here accounts for the rest, with an extra stretch round the bottom loop of the lake.

Near Howtown the lake narrows to about 400 yards (366m) at the strangely named Skelly Nab. The name derives from the freshwater herring, the schelly, found only here, in Haweswater and high up in the Red Tarn on Helvellyn. The silvery foot-long fish were once caught in nets strung between Skelly Nab and the opposite shore.

HARDY SHEEP

Ten per cent of England's sheep are in Cumbria, and the distinctive Cumbrian breed is the white-faced Herdwick. Their fleece is notable for being black when young and growing greyer with age. This hardy breed produces a hardy wool, used more for carpets than clothing. Herdwicks are known to have been here when the Romans were building Hadrian's Wall, and like the Wall they are still standing but in need of preservation. There was great concern when many of the young stock sent to winter here on lower ground were lost in the foot and mouth epidemic in 2001.

Aira Force and Dockray

This walk traverses National Trust land, via well-constructed footpaths and footbridges over Aira Beck. Starting in imposing parkland, the trail takes you past the powerful Aira Force and other waterfalls. With very little exertion you can enjoy fine views of the rushing waters, together with Ullswater and the fells in the distance.

Time: 1½ hours. Distance: 3½ miles (5.6km).
Location: Aira Force lies 2½ miles (4km) northeast of Glenridding on the A592 Windermere to Penrith road.
Start: Park at the National Trust car park at Aira Force on the A592. (OS grid ref: NY400201.)
OS Map: Outdoor Leisure 5
(The English Lakes – North Eastern area) 1:25,000.
See Key to Walks on page 121.

ROUTE DIRECTIONS

Take the path at the end of the car park through gates and into woodland. Descend towards a small stream, take the path to the left, after the hollow log, and follow the left-hand side of Aira Beck. Continue along this track next to the tree-lined ravine and pass three consecutive waterfalls of **Aira Force**. Spectacular views can be appreciated from the nearby footbridges, but do not cross them; return instead to the main path along the left side of Aira Beck and continue the walk.

As you reach the open rocky area of the third waterfall, turn left through a gap in a wall, and just beyond pass through a gate in a fence and go up a field, making sure you keep the clump of rocks on your left. At the road, turn right and follow it into Dockray (which means 'the corner of a field covered with docks'). Cross the bridge in the village, bear right, then with the Royal Hotel behind your left shoulder, take the walled path waymarked, in bushes to the right, 'Aira Force and Ulcat Row'. Follow the track and enjoy an imposing view of Gowbarrow Fell.

Keep left past the farm and other houses, then bear right to a gate and continue straight ahead. You will now have a fine view of Place Fell before you, which lies on the other side of **Ullswater**. Maintain direction into woodland and go through a gate to link up once more with Aira Beck. This time follow the other side of the ravine back past the three falls. Near the footbridge at

A rainbow hangs in the mist of water droplets above Aira Force

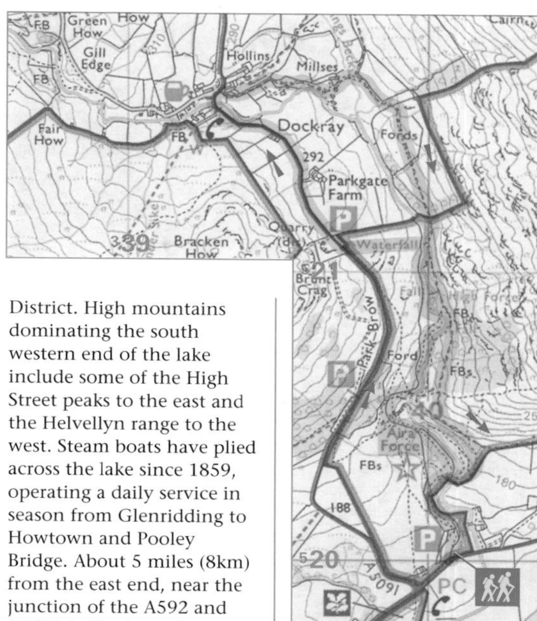

the top of Aira Force you now have a choice of two paths. From the higher route there are excellent glimpses of Ullswater, from the lower route you can enjoy views back to the main waterfall. To conclude the walk cross a footbridge and return to the car park.

POINTS OF INTEREST

Aira Force

The tumbling waterfalls at Aira Force, close to Ullswater, rarely disappoint, plunging down into a frothing pool. Bridges across the ravine allow visitors splendid views of the 70-foot (21.3-m) fall. Oaks are the native trees here and are characteristic of the hillside beside Aira Beck. Both the words, Aira and Beck, are of Scandinavian origin and mean 'gravelly stream'. The National Trust owns nearly 8,000 acres in this area.

Ullswater

At 7 miles (11.3km) long, Ullswater is the second largest lake in the Lake District. High mountains dominating the south western end of the lake include some of the High Street peaks to the east and the Helvellyn range to the west. Steam boats have plied across the lake since 1859, operating a daily service in season from Glenridding to Howtown and Pooley Bridge. About 5 miles (8km) from the east end, near the junction of the A592 and A5091 to Dockray, is Gowbarrow Park. It was here, on the shores of the lake, that Dorothy Wordsworth first saw the daffodils that her brother immortalised in his famous poem 'Daffodils'.

Looking over to the green valleys and rolling contours of remote Martindale, on the eastern shores of beautiful Ullswater

Ullswater, Penrith and the Eastern Fells

Checklist

Leisure Information
Places of Interest
Shopping
The Performing Arts
Sports, Activities and the Outdoors
Annual Events and Customs

Leisure Information

TOURIST INFORMATION CENTRES

Alston
The Railway Station. Tel: 01434 382244.

Appleby-in-Westmorland
Moot Hall, Boroughgate. Tel: 017683 51177.

Kirkby Stephen
Market Street. Tel: 017683 71199.

Penrith
Robinson's School, Middlegate. Tel: 01768 867466.

Pooley Bridge
The Square. Tel: 017684 86530.

Sedbergh
72 Main Street. Tel: 015396 20125.

Southwaite
M6 Service Area. Tel: 01697 473445/6.

Ullswater
Main Car Park, Glenridding. Tel: 017684 82414.

LAKE DISTRICT NATIONAL PARK INFORMATION POINT

Bampton
Bampton Post Office.

OTHER INFORMATION

Cumbria Wildlife Trust
Brockhole, Windermere. Tel: 015394 48280.

East Cumbria Countryside Project
Warwick Bridge, Carlisle. Tel: 01228 561601.

English Heritage
Canada House, 3 Chepstow St, Manchester. Tel: 0161 242 1400
www.english-heritage.org.uk

Lake District National Park Authority Headquarters
Murley Moss, Oxenholme Road, Kendal. Tel: 01539 724555.
www.lake-district.gov.uk

National Trust in Cumbria
The Hollens, Grasmere, Ambleside, Cumbria. Tel: 015394 35599.
www.nationaltrust.org.uk

Public Transport
The Traveline service gives details of buses, boats, trains and ferries operating throughout Cumbria. Tel: 0870 608 2608.

Weather
Lake District Weather Service. Tel: 017687 75757.

ORDNANCE SURVEY MAPS

Landranger 1:50,000 Sheets 90, 91.

The mansion of Dalemain and its wonderful gardens, near Penrith, are well worth a visit

The rocky shallows of Aira Beck, Ullswater

Outdoor Leisure 1:25,000 Sheets 5, 7.

Places of Interest

There will be an admission charge at the following places of interest unless otherwise stated.

Acorn Bank Garden
Temple Sowerby. Tel: 017683 61893. Delightful, small garden with a circular walk beside Crowdundle Beck. Extensive collection of medicinal and culinary herbs. Open Apr–Oct, daily.

Brougham Castle
Brougham. Tel: 01768 862488. Impressive remains with a keep dating from the early 13th century. Open Apr–Oct, daily.

Cumbria Police Museum
Penrith. Tel: 01768 891999. Open by appointment only.

Dalemain
Pooley Bridge, Dacre.
Tel: 017684 86450.
Delightful English country house with gardens and parkland. Open early Apr–early Oct, most days.

Hutton-in-the-Forest
Skelton. Tel: 017684 84449. Open house limited opening hours; grounds open all year, most days.

Little Salkeld Watermill
Little Salkeld, Penrith. Tel: 01768 8812523. Open all year, most days. Free.

Long Meg Stone Circle
Little Salkeld, Penrith. Open all year. Free.

Nenthead Mines Heritage Centre
Nenthead, Alston. Tel: 01434 382037. Open daily Easter–Oct.

Penrith Castle
Opposite Penrith railway station. Fourteenth-century castle.
Open all year when park is open. Free.

Penrith Museum
Robinson's School, Penrith.
Tel: 01768 212228. Open all year most days. Free.

Rheged Discovery Centre
Redhills, Penrith. This large visitor centre interprets 2,000 years of Cumbria's history and life through film and a range of innovative techniques. Restaurant, coffee shop and speciality shops. Tel: 01768 868000. Open all year, daily.

Shap Abbey
Shap. Premonstratensian abbey moved from Preston Patrick to Shap in c1199. The most striking feature is the 16th-century west tower Open any reasonable time. Free.

South Tynedale Railway
The Railway Station, Hexham Road, Alston. Tel: 01434 381696 for information about train times. Open Apr–Oct, certain days.

Wetheriggs Pottery
Wetheriggs Country Pottery, Clifton Dykes, Penrith.
Tel: 01768 892733. The UK's only remaining steam-powered pottery. Tearoom, large pottery and crafts shop. Open all year daily.

SPECIAL INTEREST FOR CHILDREN

The following places may be of interest to visitors with children. Unless otherwise stated, there will be an admission charge.

Lakeland Bird of Prey Centre
Old Walled Garden, Lowther.
Tel: 01931 712746. Daily flying demonstrations, weather permitting. Open Easter–Oct daily.

Lowther Leisure Park
Hackthorpe, near Penrith. Tel: 01931 712523. Open early Apr–end May certain days; Jun, Jul, Aug and 1st week Sep, daily.

Rheged Discovery Centre
Redhills, Penrith. Tel: 01768 868000. Open all year daily.

Wetheriggs Pottery
See pevious column.

Shopping

Appleby-in-Westmorland
Open-air market, Sat.

Penrith
Open-air market, Tue.

LOCAL SPECIALITIES

Cheese
Alston cheese, a local delicacy, can be purchased in Alston.

Cast figures
Heredities Ltd, Crossfield Mill, Kirkby Stephen. Tel: 01768 371543. Bronzed cold-cast figures.

Crafts
Gossipgate Gallery, The Butts, Alston. Tel: 01434 381806.

Mustard
Alston mustard can be purchased in Alston.

Pottery
Wetheriggs Country Pottery, Clifton Dykes, Penrith.
Tel: 01768 892733.

Schelly
Rare whitefish only found in Ullswater. On the menu at some hotels near the lake.

TURF WORK

From Harrow's Scar near Birdoswald to its end at the Solway Firth, a distance of 30 miles (48km), Hadrian's Wall was originally made of turf. Its rebuilding in stone took place partly during Hadrian's reign, and partly from AD 160. A 2-mile (3.2-km) stretch of the wall west of the River Irthing did not follow the line of the original wall, so some of the remains of the turf wall can still be seen running near by. Some of the turrets are free-standing, to enable turf ramparts to be run up them.

The old farmhouse by Birdoswald fort has been gentrified with a stepped gable over the porch and a curious battlemented extension

BIRDOSWALD Map ref NY6266

Above the dramatic Irthing Gorge, with a picnic area now looking out over it, the remote 5-acre remains of the Roman fort and settlement at Birdoswald is the most interesting spot in this western expanse of Hadrian's Wall. It was built in about the year AD 125 when its Roman name was *Banna*, and at its busiest would have housed up to 500 foot soldiers. They were there to protect this length of wall, and in particular the bridge across the River Irthing, from the Scots. Although the Wall itself is lower here than it is further east, the part of it which runs eastwards from Birdoswald towards Harrow's Scar is the longest visible remaining stretch. The mind's eye can see the rest of it snaking into the distance, a strong reminder of the scale of the project.

Of the fort itself, mainly the perimeter wall remains, with its entrance gates and part of one turret. Nevertheless, with the help of an interactive visitor centre, a vivid picture emerges of Birdoswald in Roman times. Excavations have unearthed the granaries, added in about AD 200, and other finds have included an 'Arm Purse' containing 28 silver coins, and some delicate gold jewellery now on display in Carlisle's Tullie House Museum (see page 109). A visit here is certainly recommended after seeing the site itself.

Brampton's church, with its unusual spire, features some fine Pre-Raphaelite glass

BRAMPTON Map ref NY5316

One of Cumbria's many small and attractive market towns, Brampton has held its charter since 1252. The cobbled square around the Moot Hall bustles each Wednesday, although not as much as it would have done in 1745 when Brampton was the headquarters of Bonnie Prince Charlie's army while it was laying siege to Carlisle Castle. Worth seeking out is St Martin's Church, which has some excellent stained-glass windows made by William Morris and designed by Burne-Jones.

The Augustinian Priory at Lanercost, in a delightful wooded valley two miles (3.2km) northeast of Brampton, was dedicated to St Mary Magdalene in 1169. Although much of it is in ruins, including the main priory buildings, the nave of the church still survives and has been used as the local parish church from the mid 1700s to the present day. Its vaulted ceilings are splendid, and it is a great shame that its location, close to the Scottish border, made it the subject of Scottish raids over the centuries, hastening its downfall. Inevitably, Robert the Bruce was one of the culprits, as too was William Wallace (portrayed by Mel Gibson in the 1995 film *Braveheart.*)

WILLIAM WALLACE

William 'Braveheart' Wallace, who is known to have raided Lanercost Priory, was born in about the year 1274. He was an early campaigner for Scottish independence from the English who ruled the country at the time. He was a man who believed in action, too. In 1297 he killed the English sheriff in Lanark, then defeated Edward I's army at Stirling Bridge and began moving into northern England. By 1298, however, Edward I's troops fought back and defeated Wallace at Falkirk. After escaping to France he returned to Scotland but was arrested in 1305. That same year he was hanged, drawn and quartered in London, the quarters of his body being sent to Newcastle, Berwick, Stirling and Perth.

CARLISLE Map ref NY3956

If you want to begin with the history of Carlisle, then a visit to the award-winning Tullie House Museum and Art Gallery in Castle Street with its interactive displays is the place to start. It traces the history of Carlisle from before the Romans to the railways and beyond, via the reivers, Robert the Bruce and the Roundheads. It also has very good natural history displays, including an illuminated microscope which is very popular with children. Indeed, a great deal of thought has gone into all the exhibits,

Gay flower beds grace the gardens beside Carlisle's new Sands Centre

which combine education and entertainment. You can try writing on Roman wax tablets, have a go on a crossbow, walk through a mine tunnel or check if you might be descended from a reiver. If your name is Armstrong, note that a never-repealed anti-reiver statute requires all Armstrongs to be outside the city gates by curfew time!

Linked to the museum by the Millennium Gallery, Carlisle Castle originally dates from 1092 when the first castle on this site was built by William II. Most of the buildings today are from these times. There are several rooms decorated in medieval style in the gatehouse, while inside the castle there is a warren of chambers and passageways to explore. The castle was captured by Bonnie Prince Charlie in 1745, and Mary, Queen of Scots was once imprisoned here. Also here is the Museum of the Border Regiment; while it is mainly of interest to military historians, its collection of weaponry, uniforms, medals and other items also reveal many tragic and heroic stories from the wars in which the Regiment has been involved. Our Walk on page 114 starts at the castle.

In 1122, 30 years after the castle was built, Carlisle Cathedral was founded. It was originally a priory but became a cathedral under Henry I in 1132 and can claim to have had a daily service for almost 900 years. Inside, the first thing to strike the eye is the magnificent high ceiling, with bright blue panels and golden stars. Its stained glass ranges from the 14th to the 20th centuries, the oldest being in the East Window. On no account miss seeing the buildings opposite the cathedral's main entrance. The Fratry was originally a 13th-century

CURIOUS CARLISLE

Carlisle is, by area, the largest city in England and, in Cold Fell, at 2,041 feet (622m), has the highest point in any English city. Thanks to Mary, Queen of Scots, it claims the first international football match. Outside the Old Town Hall visitor centre, a Victorian pillar box commemorates that this is where England's first pillar box stood.

monastic common room and now contains the cathedral library and the Prior's Kitchen Restaurant. Across from the Fratry is the 13th-century Prior's Tower, used, amongst other things, as a place of refuge from the reivers and other Scottish raiders. Inside the Prior's Tower, which can be seen by arrangement (or if you ask one of the cathedral guides when they're not too busy), is a ceiling containing 45 panels, hand-painted in 1510.

Slightly overshadowed by the cathedral but worth a visit in its own right is St Cuthbert's Church, which was also originally built in the 12th century although the present buildings date from the 1700s. Its most unusual feature is a moveable pulpit, mounted on rail tracks, while the nearby tithe barn can be visited on request. This was used to house the tithes or taxes, paid in the form of wool, grain or straw, by the people of Carlisle.

The city walls around Carlisle give some idea of the extent of the place in Roman times, as they were built – some 1,000 years after Hadrian's Wall – around the remains of the Roman town and fort. The West Walls, which run behind St Cuthbert's and around the cathedral, are the best surviving examples. These were begun in 1122 but not completed until the year 1200.

Carlisle's timber-framed Guildhall was built in 1404 and now houses the Guildhall Museum. It tells partly of local history but also the stories behind the guilds which have used the building from the 15th century to the present day. The Guild of Shoemakers still use the Shoemakers' Room for its meetings. Other displays cover the Weavers, Tanners, Merchants and Butchers.

Other notable buildings include the Citadel (a never-completed fortress begun in 1541) and the 18th-century Town Hall which is now used as a visitor centre.

THE REIVERS

From the 14th to the late 17th centuries, the lands around Carlisle, on the hazy border between England and Scotland, were a lawless place. Villainous families took advantage of this, raiding homes and villages under cover of darkness, stealing cattle and sometimes murdering their victims. There are 77 names on record as belonging to these disreputable reiver families, amongst them the names of Trotter and Maxwell. There was even a reiving thieving season, beginning in August, by which time the cattle were well-fed and healthy, and lasting for three months, until the nearest law courts reconvened. From Archbold to Young, the reiver names are recorded in Carlisle's Tullie House Museum.

In the 16th century the rent payable by families and farmers to the landowners was known as greenmail. The reivers demanded that those same families paid them protection money if they wished to be allowed to live on the land in peace. Because of this underhand method, and the fact that the reivers often came by night, the term 'blackmail' was used to describe the money they extracted by threats.

Carlisle's 17th-century market cross boasts a four-faced sundial and a crowned lion

The Reivers' Tour

During the 16th century this area of the Scottish–English border was one of the most lawless places in Britain. Reivers were the people who lived on either side of the border and who plundered each other's property and cattle, killing each other into the bargain. Today the quiet, beautiful countryside gives no indication as to the hell on earth this area must have been for its inhabitants. Reiving has left its dreadful mark on the English language with the word 'bereaved'.

ROUTE DIRECTIONS

See Key to Car Tours on page 120.

The length of this tour is 68 miles (109km), it begins at Carlisle, the county town of Cumbria and the largest city in the area. There has been a settlement here since Celtic times, followed by the Romans, the Romano-Celts, Saxons, Danes, Normans, Scots and English. Carlisle's imposing **Castle**, which now houses a **Regimental Museum**, is a reminder of this constant conflict. The cathedral, built by the Normans, is also an indication of their search for peace after creating mayhem in the district, as they did in the rest of Britain. Visit the Reivers Exhibition at Tullie House to gain an accurate picture of the time and events of the reivers before starting out on your journey into the past.

Leave Carlisle on the A7. Drive round Hardwicke Circus roundabout and cross the River Eden. Shortly go right along the B6264 towards Hexham and Newcastle. This is the area through which cattle, sheep and vegetables were brought to Carlisle. As Carlisle had been the traditional market centre for miles around and as roads were practically non-existent, the people had very little choice of where they could go to get the best prices.

Cross the M6 and meet a roundabout, where you take the 2nd exit on to the A689. Just past Carlisle Airport, turn left on to an unclassified road to Irthington. You are now on the old Stanegate Roman road. Irthington is one of the villages that was badly affected by reiving. Today only a mound is evidence of the Norman castle that once stood here.

About a mile (1.6km) after Irthington, turn right on the A6071 and after crossing the bridge, turn left to Walton. The name Walton is a reminder that British/Welsh

To the east of Carlisle the River Eden meanders slowly through lush meadowland

people continued living here when the Anglo-Saxons had settled in the area (*wal* or *wealas* was the Saxon word for foreigner). It is a very small village with lovely views of the Irthing Valley. (Eden and Irthing come from the same Celtic word, meaning 'to gush'.)

Keep forward through Walton and at the junction with the B6318 turn right, signposted 'Gilsland and Greenhead'. Just after a mile (1.6km) turn left for Askerton Castle and Bewcastle church. At Bewcastle turn right up to the church and the cross.

Bewcastle is very close to the Scottish border and this proximity was one of the reasons that made it the focus for reiving activity and there were many tracks leading through the area. In 1582 Thomas Musgrave, Captain of Bewcastle, and his tenants lost 700 cattle, 300 sheep, and crops and buildings were burnt. The history of Bewcastle goes back much further – to Celtic and Roman times. During the 2nd and 3rd centuries AD there were around 1,000 Roman soldiers stationed here. In the churchyard the Bewcastle Cross is an excellent example of Anglo-Saxon sculpture and a very early Christian memorial, as the majority of Saxons were still pagans at this time. During the time of the reivers, it was said that only women were buried in the churchyard, all the men were hanged in Carlisle.

At Bewcastle, turn left, then at the next junction take the right fork. Turn right at the T-junction on to the B6318, which bears left. Continue for 4 miles (6.4km) to where the B6318 turns left once again. Do not take this left turn but continue straight ahead on a minor road, then bear right at

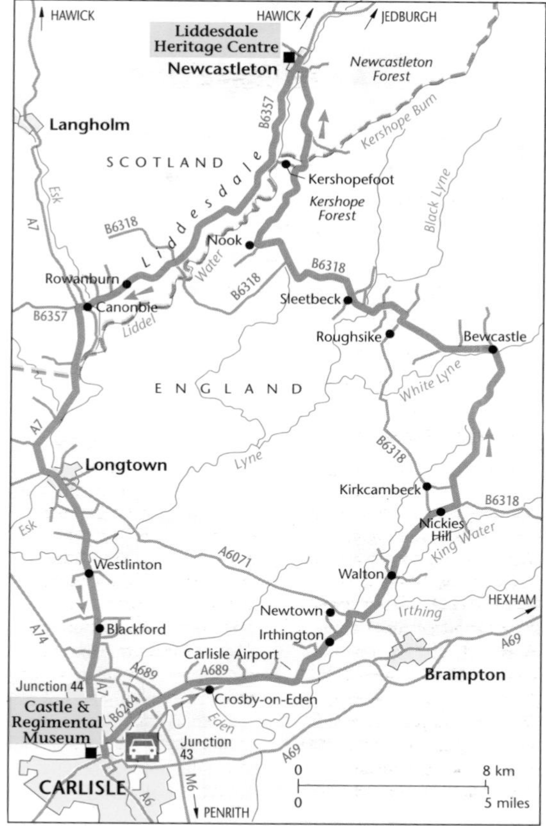

the next junction, heading for Newcastleton. You are now in Scotland. In Newcastleton take the opportunity to stop for a snack and visit the **Liddesdale Heritage Centre**.

Return south on the B6357 and after Canonbie join the A7 to return to England and Carlisle.

A handsome old pillar-box stands outside Carlisle's Tourist Information Centre

East (and West) of Eden

It is difficult to imagine, on this easy family walk, that Carlisle was the scene of so much strife for so many centuries. It was important as a military position for the Iron-Age Celts, the Romans and also during the Dark Ages and Middle Ages. This leisurely walk will give you a feeling of tranquillity and history in this celebrated city.

Time: 1½ hours. Distance: 3 miles (4.8km).
Location: Carlisle. Situated 2 miles (3.2km) off the M6 (junction 43), 10 miles (16km) south of the Scottish border.
Start: Carlisle Castle in the city centre. Car parks at both sides of the Castle. (OS grid ref: NY396561.)
OS Map: Explorer 315 (Carlisle) 1:25,000.
See Key to Walks page 121.

ROUTE DIRECTIONS

Both an underpass and the Millennium Gallery, an underground gallery by the start of the walk, link Tullie House to the 11th-century Carlisle Castle.

Facing the castle gate turn left along the dual carriageway (Castle Way), walk below the stark Millennium Bridge and turn right. This will lead you alongside the west wall of Carlisle Castle and the River Caldew to the River Eden. Where the road bears right take the left-hand fork, the park road, which leads around the circumference of Bitts Park, through the trees to reach a bridge near the confluence of the Caldew and the Eden. Do not cross the bridge, but turn right; along this part of the walk you can see the houses of Stanwix through the trees on the opposite bank.

Turn left near the tennis courts and follow the path which goes under the A7 road bridge, ascend to your right then turn right to cross the river, then right again through the gardens into Rickerby Park which was bought by the city as a memorial to those who died in World War I. As the river meanders first north and then south you will have excellent views of the city's skyline – the Civic Centre, cathedral, Dixon's Chimney and the castle.

After passing the war memorial, recross the river via the memorial suspension bridge. Turn right and follow the river back under the A7 bridge again and turn left on a path which diagonally crosses Bitts Park with tennis courts on your right. Cross the road and take the footpath to meet up with Castle Way at the eastern corner of the castle. Walk through the underpass (located opposite the Gatehouse) and beneath the dual carriageway to reach the bottom of Castle Street. Mid-way along Castle Street is the unassuming Norman cathedral. Return to the castle car park and the start point of this walk.

Carlisle's old town hall, with clock tower and a gilded weather vane, is now home to the Tourist Information Centre

POINTS OF INTEREST

Carlisle Castle

Cumbria's county town first began to develop as a Roman town in the 1st century BC. Carlisle developed further as a frontier town when Hadrian's Wall was built to

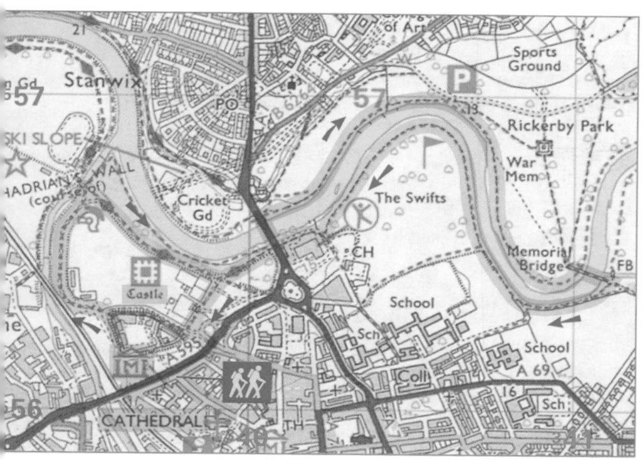

Carlisle Cathedral
This Norman building, constructed in 1122, is England's second smallest cathedral. It preserves one of the finest east windows in the country, superb carved choir stalls and a painted barrel-vaulted ceiling.

River Eden
The name for the River Eden comes from the Celtic 'to gush'; however by the time it has reached Carlisle the river has slowed down considerably.

control the northern boundary of the Empire. The castle, built by William Rufus in 1092, and strengthened by David I of Scotland, was for centuries the centre of conflicts between the Scottish and English; the Scots, just prior to the defeat of Bonnie Prince Charlie, were finally ousted in 1745. The fine 12th-century keep and the 14th-century main gates are the most impressive surviving buildings of the castle. The Border Regiment Museum is housed in the inner ward.

Tullie House Museum and Art Gallery
An award-winning museum that traces the history of Carlisle and the Border country back 2,000 years. The turbulent and violent history unfolds before you via novel and unusual settings and displays, which involve climbing part of Hadrian's turf wall and experiencing a land inhabited by eagles and peregrines.

The city's 19th-century citadel formerly housed the law courts

HADRIAN

Hadrian was born in AD 76 and was Emperor from AD 117, until his death in AD 138. The Wall across the north of England was just one of the projects by which he marked the limits of the Roman Empire's expansion, and a consolidation of its borders. In addition to writing prose and poetry in both Latin and Greek (he had lived in Athens prior to becoming Emperor) he was passionate about architecture. Apart from Hadrian's Wall he was also responsible for Hadrian's Arch in Athens and both the original Pantheon and the Athenaeum in Rome.

HADRIAN'S WALL

In about AD 121, the Roman soldiers stationed in northern England began to build a wall that was to run for 73 miles (116.8km) from the Solway Firth to the River Tyne in the east. Working under the instructions of the Emperor Hadrian (AD 76–138), the soldiers laboured with stones and masonry to produce a barrier which would keep out the wild tribes of northern Britain, while Rome tried to civilise the English behind the wall by introducing such modern features as central heating, public baths and an efficient drainage system.

There are several examples of such Roman remains at various places along the wall, though the finest examples – Chesters, Corbridge, Vindolanda and Housesteads – are to the east of the area covered in this book. In addition to the fort at Birdoswald (see page 108), there are some parts of the western section of Hadrian's Wall that are well worth visiting. There are the remains – some of them substantial – of turrets at Piper Sike, Leahill and Banks East, while at Hare Hill, near Lanercost, is a section of the wall some 9 feet (2.7m) in height. At Dovecote Bridge, near Brampton, is a unique section of Hadrian's Wall, the only stretch that was built from Cumbrian red sandstone. Unfortunately, to preserve it from erosion and damage, this section of the wall has been covered over by earth. Such care does need to be taken with the Wall, the whole of which has been declared a World Heritage Site by UNESCO.

Years of hard labour must have gone into the building of the Emperor Hadrian's great wall

Carlisle and the Borderlands

Leisure Information
Places of Interest
Shopping
The Performing Arts
Sports, Activities
and the Outdoors
Annual Events and Customs

Leisure Information

TOURIST INFORMATION CENTRES

Brampton
Moot Hall, Market Square.
Tel: 016977 3433.

Carlisle
The Old Town Hall. Tel: 01228 625600.

Longtown
3 HIgh Street. Tel: 01228 792835.

OTHER INFORMATION

Cumbria Wildlife Trust
Brockhole, Windermere.
Tel: 015394 48280.

English Heritage
Canada House, 3 Chepstow St, Manchester. Tel: 0161 242 1400
www.english-heritage.org.uk

National Trust in Cumbria
The Hollens, Grasmere, Ambleside, Cumbria.
Tel: 015394 35599.
www.nationaltrust.org.uk

Parking
Carlisle city centre is a designated parking disc zone, with free parking in some streets. Discs are obtainable free from the Civic Centre, Visitor Centre, Police Station, traffic wardens and many shops, banks and offices. Disc parking areas are indicated by road markings and signs, giving details of time limits.

Public Transport
The Traveline service gives details of buses, boats, trains and ferries operating throughout Cumbria.Tel: 0870 608 2608.

Weather
Lake District Weather Service.
Tel: 017687 75757.

ORDNANCE SURVEY MAPS

Landranger 1:50,000
Sheet 85.
Explorer 1:25,000 Sheet 315.

Places of Interest

There will be an admission charge at the following places of interest unless otherwise stated.

Bewcastle Cross
Bewcastle. Open all year, daily. Free.

Birdoswald Roman Fort
Gilsland, near Carlisle.

Peaceful Brampton was occupied by the rebellious Jacobite army in 1745

The dramatic ruins of Lanercost Priory date back to the 12th century

Tel: 016977 47602. Dating from AD 125, the fort housed up to 500 Roman soldiers stationed on Hadrian's Wall. The perimeter wall, entrance gates and one turret can be seen. There is an interactive visitor centre on the site. Open Easter–Oct daily; winter opening by appointment only.

Border Regiment and King's Own Royal Border Regiment Museum
Queen Mary's Tower, The Castle, Carlisle. Tel: 01228 532774. Trophies, models, pictures and silver tell the story of the regiment. Open all year, most days.

Carlisle Castle
Castle Way, Carlisle. Medieval castle captured by Bonnie Prince Charlie in 1745. Houses a regimental museum (see above). Tel: 01228 591922. Open all year, daily.

Guildhall Museum
Green Market, Carlisle. Tel: 01228 534781. Local history displays and the stories behind the local Guilds. Open Apr–Oct, certain afternoons.

Lanercost Priory
Tel: 016977 3030. Augustinian Priory in a delightful wooded valley 2 miles (3.2km) north-east of Brampton. The main priory buildings are in ruins, but the nave of the church survives and is now the local parish church. Open Apr–Sep daily.

Settle–Carlisle Railway
Scenic 72-mile (115.2-km) route. For further details about the special steam trips which run occasionally along the line as well as the standard trains, contact the local Tourist Information Centre or Tel: 01729 82503.

Tullie House Museum and Art Gallery
Castle Street, Carlisle. Tel: 01228 534781. Interactive displays trace the history of Carlisle, including the Romans, the reivers, Robert the Bruce, and the Roundheads. Natural history displays. Open all year, most days.

SPECIAL INTEREST FOR CHILDREN

The following places may be of interest to visitors with children. Unless otherwise stated, there will be an admission charge.

Settle–Carlisle Railway
Scenic 72-mile (115.2-km) route. For details see entry in previous column.

Tullie House Museum and Art Gallery
Castle Street, Carlisle. For details see entry in previous column.

Shopping

Brampton
Market, Wed.

Carlisle
Market, Mon to Sat.

LOCAL SPECIALITIES

Ice-creams and sorbets
Cumbrian Cottage, Gelt House Farm, Hayton, Carlisle. Tel: 01228 670296.

Trout
New Mills Trout Farm, Brampton. Tel: 016977 2384. Fish and other local produce in farm shop.

Woollens
Eden Valley Woollen Mills, Front Street, Armathwaite, Carlisle. Tel: 016974 572457.
Linton Visitors' Centre (hand looms) Shaddongate, Carlisle. Tel: 01228 527569.

The Performing Arts

Sands Centre
Carlisle. Tel: 01228 625222.
Stanwix Arts Theatre
Brampton Road, Carlisle.
Tel: 01228 400300.

Sports, Activities and the Outdoors

ANGLING

Fly
Lough Trout Fishery, Thurstonfield, Carlisle.
Tel: 01228 576552.
New Mills Trout Farm, near Brampton.
Tel: 016977 2384.

CYCLE HIRE

Brampton
Pedal Pushers.
Tel: 016977 42387.

GOLF COURSES

Brampton
Brampton Golf Course, Talkin Tarn. Tel: 016977 2255/2000.
Carlisle
Carlisle Golf Club, Aglionby.
Tel: 01228 513303.
Stony Holme, St Aidans Road.
Tel: 01228 625511.

GUIDED WALKS

Carlisle
Guided city walks. Details from Carlisle Tourist Information Centre. Charge.

HORSE-RACING

Carlisle Racecourse, Durdar Road. Tel: 01228 522973.

HORSE-RIDING

Brampton
Bailey Mill Farm, near Brampton.
Tel: 016977 2384.
Carlisle
Blackdyke Farm, Blackford.
Tel: 01228 674633. Cargo Riding Centre, Cargo. Tel: 01228 674300. Stonerigg Riding Centre, The Bow, Great Orton.
Tel: 01228 576232.

LONG-DISTANCE FOOTPATHS AND TRAILS

Cumbria Way
Carlisle and Ulverston are linked by this 70-mile (113km) route through the Lake District.
The Settle to Carlisle Walk
A 151-mile (241.6-km) walk from Settle, in North Yorkshire, to Carlisle.

RUGBY

Carlisle
Carlisle Rugby Union Club, Warwick Road. Tel: 01228 521300.

WATERSPORTS

Brampton
Talkin Tarn Country Park. Canoeing, rowing, sailing and windsurfing are available at Talkin Tarn.
Tel: 016977 3129.

Annual Events and Customs

Bewcastle
Bewcastle Sports (including sheepdog trials), late August.
Brampton
Brampton Sheepdog Trials, mid-September.
Carlisle
Carlisle and Borders Spring Show, early May.
Penton Sheepdog Trials, late May.
Carlisle Carnival, mid-June.
Cumberland Show, mid-July.

The checklists give details of some of the facilities within the area covered by this guide. Further information can be obtained from Tourist Information Centres.

Carlisle's ancient castle has witnessed turbulent events in the town's history

Atlas and Map Symbols

THE NATIONAL GRID SYSTEM

The National Grid system covers Great Britain with an imaginary network of 100 kilometre grid squares. Each square is given a unique alphabetic reference as shown in the diagram. These squares are sub-divided into one hundred 10 kilometre squares, each numbered from 0 to 9 in an easterly (left to right) direction and northerly (upwards) direction from the bottom left corner. Each 10 km square is similarly sub-divided into one hundred 1 km squares.

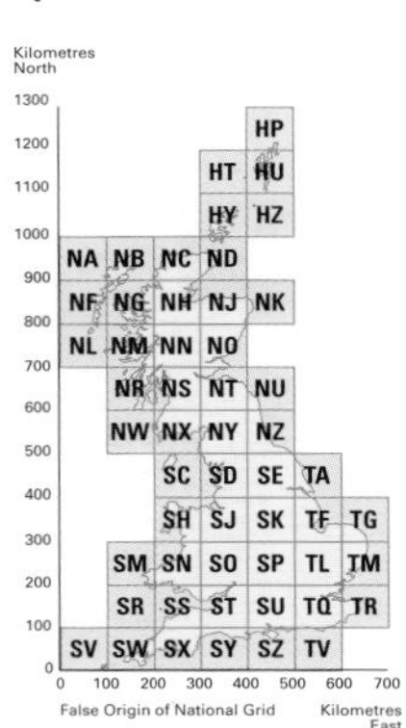

KEY TO ATLAS

	MOTORWAY		A ROAD
M4	Motorway with number	A1123	Other A road single/dual carriageway
Fleet	Motorway service area		Road tunnel
11	Motorway junction with and without number	Toll	Toll
3	Restricted motorway junctions		Road under construction
	Motorway and junction under construction		Roundabout
	PRIMARY ROUTE		B ROAD
A3	Primary route single/dual carriageway	B2070	B road single/dual carriageway
Grantham North	Primary route service area		B road interchange junction
BATH	Primary route destinations		B road roundabout with adjoining unclassified road
	Roundabout		Steep gradient
5	Distance in miles between symbols		Unclassified road single/dual carriageway
	Narrow Primary route with passing places		Railway station and level crossing

KEY TO ATLAS

	Abbey, cathedral or priory		National trail
	Aquarium	NT	National Trust property
	Castle	NTS	National Trust for Scotland property
	Cave		Nature reserve
	Country park		Other place of interest
	County cricket ground	P+R	Park and Ride location
	Farm or animal centre		Picnic site
	Forest drive		Steam centre
	Garden		Ski slope natural
	Golf course		Ski slope artifical
	Historic house		Tourist Information Centre
	Horse racing		Viewpoint
	Motor racing		Visitor or heritage centre
	Museum		Zoological or wildlife collection
	AA telephone		Forest Park
	Airport		Heritage coast
	Heliport		National Park (England & Wales)
	Windmill		National Scenic Area (Scotland)

KEY TO TOURS

	Tour start point	Buckland Abbey	Highlighted point of interest
	Direction of tour		Featured tour
	Optional detour		

KEY TO WALKS

Scale 1:25,000, 2½ inches to 1 mile, 4cm to 1 km

- Start of walk
- Direction of walk
- Line of walk
- Optional detour
- Buckland Abbey — Highlighted point of interest

ROADS AND PATHS

M1 or A6(M)	M1 or A6(M)	Motorway
A 31(T) or A35	A 31(T) or A35	Trunk or main road
B 3074	B 3074	Secondary road
A 35	A 35	Dual carriageway
		Road generally more than 4m wide
		Road generally less than 4m wide
		Other road, drive or track
		Path

Unfenced roads and tracks are shown by pecked lines

RAILWAYS

- Multiple track } Standard gauge
- Single track } Standard gauge
- Narrow gauge
- Siding
- Cutting
- Embankment
- Tunnel
- Road over; road under
- Level crossing
- Station

PUBLIC RIGHTS OF WAY

Public rights of way may not be evident on the ground

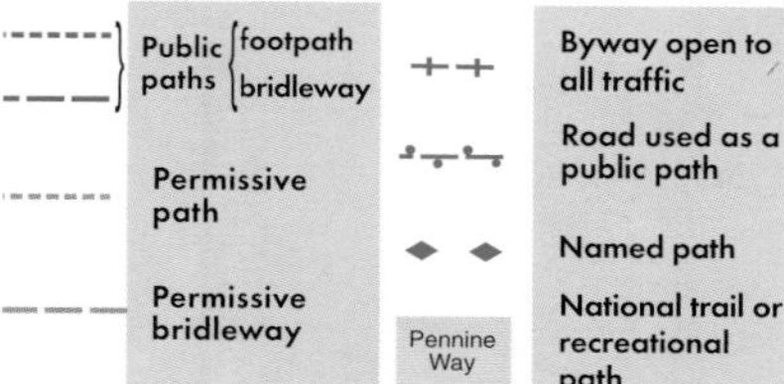

The representation on this map of any other road, track or path is no evidence of the existence of a right of way

RELIEF

50 ·	Heights determined by	Ground survey
285 ·		Air survey

Contours are at 5 and 10 metres vertical interval

SYMBOLS

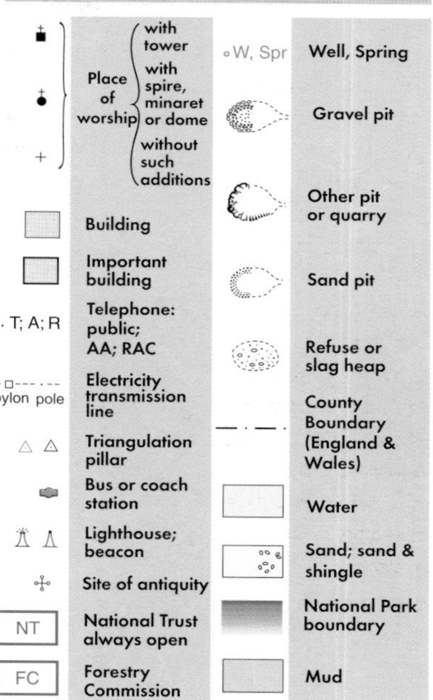

DANGER AREA

Firing and test ranges in the area
Danger!
Observe warning notices

VEGETATION

Limits of vegetation are defined by positioning of the symbols but may be delineated also by pecks or dots

- Coniferous trees
- Non-coniferous trees
- Orchard
- Heath
- Coppice
- Marsh, reeds, saltings.

TOURIST AND LEISURE INFORMATION

- Camp site
- Information centre
- Information centre (seasonal)
- Caravan site
- Picnic site
- PC — Public convenience
- P — Parking
- Viewpoint
- Mountain rescue post

Workington
Whitehaven
Cockermouth
Keswick
Egremont
Cleator Moor
Millom
Ulverston
BARROW-IN-FURNESS
Dalton-in-Furness
Ravenglass
Seascale
Gosforth
St Bees
St Bees Head
Broughton-in-Furness
Coniston
Grasmere
Bassenthwaite
Threlkeld
Braithwaite
Portinscale
Buttermere
Loweswater
Lamplugh
Rosthwaite
Seatoller
Wasdale Head
Nether Wasdale
Eskdale
Boot
Bootle
Whitbeck
Silecroft
Haverigg
Askam in Furness
Kirkby-in-Furness
Greenodd
Rampside
ISLE OF WALNEY
LAKE DISTRICT
LAKE DISTRICT NATIONAL PARK
CUMBRIAN MOUNTAINS
Furness Fells
978 SCAFELL PIKE
964 SCAFELL
931 SKIDDAW
899 GREAT GABLE
892 PILLAR
0 1 2 3 miles
0 1 2 3 4 5 kilometres

Penrith
Kendal
Windermere
Kirkby Lonsdale
Morecambe
Appleby-in-Westmorland
Shap
Tebay
Orton
Sedbergh
Ambleside
Patterdale
Pooley Bridge
Ullswater
Haweswater
Grange-over-Sands
Carnforth
Ingleton
Kirkby Stephen
Milburn Forest
Dufton Fell
Lune Forest
Langdale
Garsdale
Long Sleddale
Milnthorpe
Staveley
Burneside
Oxenholme
Bowness-on-Windermere
Troutbeck
Kentmere
Bampton
Askham
Clifton
Eamont Bridge
Yanwath
Stainton
Dacre
Greystoke
Skelton
Langwathby
Culgaith
Kirkby Thore
Brough
Ravenstonedale
Dent
Barbon
Casterton
High Bentham
Clapham
Austwick
Hornby
Bolton le Sands
Arnside
Silverdale
Levens
Crook
Winster
Sawrey
Lindale
Beetham
Holme
Burton-in-Kendal
Whittington
Tunstall
Wray
Wennington
Shap Summit
High Street
High Raise
Ingleborough Hill
Whernside
The Calf
Wild Boar Fell
Cross Fell
Great Dun Fell

Hermitage
Riccarton
Newlands
568
ROAN FELL
521
ARKLETON HILL
Steele Road
403
LOCH KNOWE
Kielder
Kielder Castle
MONKSIDE
397
EARLS SEAT
Kielder Water
Liddel Water
B6399
B6357
Castleton
413
WILSON'S PIKE
Black Middens Bastle House
307
WHITE HILL
Gatehouse
Newcastleton
LIDDESDALE
Falstone
Tower Knowe
Stannersburn
Greenhaugh
Hott
404
TINNIS HILL
GLENDHU HILL
275
BLINKBONNY HEIGHT
Kershope Burn
Lewis Burn
Border Forest Park
Under Burnmouth
NORTHUMBERLAND
NATIONAL PARK
519
SIGHTY CRAG
492
BLACK KNOWE
395
BOLTS LAW
Caulside
B6357
Claygate
Rowanburn
Canonbie
Pentonbridge
355
BARRON'S PIKE
313
SPY RIGG
325
ROUND TOP
B6318
Bewcastle
Black Fell
265
GREEN RIGG
River Irthing
Greenlee Lough
Broomlee Lough
Housesteads Fort NT
B6318
River Lyne
Boltonfellend
Kirkcambeck
Kirklinton
Hethersgill
Hadrian's Wall
B6318
Gilsland
Greenhead
Chesterholm (Vindolanda)
Smithfield
A6071
Walton
Haltwhistle
Henshaw
Thorngrafton
Bardon Mill
Scalebyhill
Scaleby
Burtholme
A69
Melkridge
Beltingham
Laversdale
Newtown
Crooked Holme
R Irthing
Lanercost
Low Row
255
DENTON FELL
Oldwall
Brampton
Irthington
Deanraw
Milton
Park
Rowfoot
Low Crosby
A689
High Crosby
Newby East
Hallbankgate
Tindale
A689
Coanwood
Fellhouse Fell
Linstock
R Eden
Farlam
Halton Lea Gate
Lambley
Whitfield
CARLISLE
A69
Hayton
Talkin
Talkin Tarn
How Mill
Warwick
Eals
Scotby
Fenton
Heads Nook
621
COLD FELL
522
GLENDUE FELL
Castle Carrock
River Gelt
Harraby
Wetheral
Great Corby
Wetheral Priory Gatehouse
Knarsdale
M6
Upperby
Cumwhinton
B6413
B6263
R South Tyne
Ninebanks
Cumwhitton
483
CUMREW FELL
521
GELTSDALE MIDDLE
584
THREE PIKES
Slaggyford
A686
Cotehill
River Eden
Cumrew
Kirkhaugh
Newbiggin
South Tynedale Railway
R West Allen
A689
Wreay
Croglin
Croglin Water
657
MIDDLE CARRICK
572
HARTLEY MOOR
Carr Shield
Low Hesket
Aiketgate
Ainstable
Alston
B6294
Southwaite
Armathwaite
559
RENWICK FELL
664
BLACK FELL
Gilderdale Forest
High Hesket
B6413
Ivegill
Renwick
Nenthead
R Petteril
High Bankhill
624
HARTSIDE HEIGHT
627
Killhope Summit
Killhope Lead Mining Centre
Staffield
A6
M6
580
Hartside Summit
Shield Water
A686
Kirkoswald
Garrigill
Calthwaite
Lazonby
Gamblesby
Roe Beck
Hutton End
Glassonby
247
LAZONBY FELL
710
MELMERBY FELL
B6277
747
BURNHOPE SEAT
B6413
Salkeld Dykes
Great Salkeld
Long Meg and her Daughters
Melmerby
Plumpton
R South Tyne
Hutton-in-the-Forest
Ellonby
Skelton
Little Salkeld
Hunsonby
740
GREEN FELL
B6412
Winskill
Ousby
893
CROSS FELL
Little Blencow
Catterlen
B5305
Langwathby
Skirwith
Milburn Forest
Trout Beck
Crowdundle Beck
Johnby
Great Blencow
847
GREAT DUN FELL
Edenhall
357
BERRIER HILL
Greystoke
Newton Reigny
Penrith
A686
Blencarn
Cow Green Reservoir
B5288
R Eamont
B6412
Motherby
Newbiggin
Brougham
Culgaith
Milburn
Penruddock
A66
Stainton
Rheged Discovery Centre
Countess Pillar
Eamont Bridge
220
Temple Sowerby
Newbiggin
Acorn Bank NT
Dufton Fell
Cauldron Snout (Waterfall)
Dalemain
Yanwath
Knock
Pennine Way
Dacre
Tirril
Clifton
River Eden
Kirkby Thore
481
DUFTON PIKE
Maize Beck
536
GREAT MELL FELL
B5320
Lowther
Melkinthorpe
Cliburn
Long Marton
Dufton
672
MURTON FELL

Index